GOING INTO THERAPY

Going into Therapy

TED CLARK

PERENNIAL LIBRARY
Harper & Row, Publishers
New York, Evanston, San Francisco, London

For information address Harper & Row, Publishers, Inc., 10 East 53d Street, New York, N.Y. 10022. Published simultaneously in Canada by Fitzhenry & Whiteside Limited, Toronto.

First PERRENIAL LIBRARY edition published 1975.

LIBRARY OF CONGRESS CATALOG CARD NUMBER: 74-25154

STANDARD BOOK NUMBER: 06-080347-9

Contents

Preface

Many people go into psychotherapy without considering the complex and possibly risky nature of the decisions which must be made concerning therapy. This problem is a murky one because there are few definitive answers to any question concerning psychotherapy. Yet, to avoid wasting time or ending up with an inappropriate therapy, some attention must be paid by therapists and clients to guidelines. The purpose of this book is not to provide answers; ultimately any answers must come from the individual and reflect his or her point of view. The purpose is to outline the questions involved, explore the relevant issues, and offer suggestions which may be helpful in clarifying the process and allowing people more control over their own lives.

1
Why Go into Therapy?

Why do you want to get into psychotherapy? What do you want from therapy? Knowing the answers to these questions before you enter a therapy relationship will help you select a therapist and an approach to therapy which will be appropiate to your needs. Unsatisfying, even hurtful situations often result when a person enters therapy blindly. Such "leaps of faith" may be motivated by a desperate need for immediate relief from suffering, a belief that the professional status of the therapist ensures he or she will be competent, trustworthy, and responsible, or simply a resigned attitude which leaves the outcome of the choice to get into therapy up to fate. Certainly the decision to enter therapy is not a simple one to make, but if a person is able to make an informed, insightful, and conscious decision about when to enter therapy, with whom, to do what, for specific goals, the entire process will be more meaningful and helpful.

People get into therapy in three ways. First, they choose to go for themselves. Second, they go because someone close to them (a husband, wife, child, parent) refuses to go alone but seems to be having problems he or she needs help to resolve which affect the individual. Finally, the individual may be forced to go into therapy by well-meaning relatives, spouses, or authority figures. Involuntary treatment is rarely helpful: usually people coerced into therapy resist help, are brutalized by the pressures, and suffer emotional damage. Therefore, this book will focus on voluntary psychotherapy.

The decision to get into therapy is different for each individual who makes it. However, we can divide the general approaches to therapy into four, not necessarily exclusive, categories: therapy focusing on personality or identity problems; crisis intervention, family (or interpersonal) approaches, and therapy or group experiences for the purpose of personal growth.

A crisis is simply a turning point. Everyone experiences many crises in his or her life, but occasionally the crisis is the culmination of many converging factors the person is only partially aware of and does not feel control over. The result is a state of fear, aggressiveness, helplessness, contradictions, and vulnerability. The individual searches for help, first among friends or relatives, then from "professionals."

Ann believed she was deeply in love with Al. He was almost telepathically sensitive to her needs and feelings. Despite his past record in relationships—he had left many women—she was sure she was different and that he needed this difference. Her work improved as the relationship boosted her morale, and she began making many new friends. Al was all she needed, she felt, to be a whole person. Suddenly Al was no longer completely available to her. She denied any lack of intensity in his attentions, pointing out that she, too, was very busy. Suddenly Al announced he had found a new lover. Ann was shattered. She attempted to hold in her grief, to dissemble. No one must know how hurt she felt, as this would humiliate her, make it seem as if she were unloveable. Her work declined, although she believed this was because of her employer's unreasonable demands. Her friends offered emotional support, but she interpreted it as concealed glee at her inability to hold Al's love. After a month of severe depression (loss of appetite, heavy sleeping, listlessness, a sense of impending doom) Ann was persuaded to see a therapist. She insisted nothing was wrong with her, that she didn't need any help, but she came to please her friends.

Ann's situation is a typical example of a personal crisis: a sudden loss precipitated extreme emotional distress. The ripple effect created the impression to Ann that her whole world was falling apart and distracted her from her true loss, her relationship with Al. In therapy, as this loss was explored and similar losses in her past were compared with it, Ann realized she had been reenacting her father's rejection of her when she was little, and the depression following her loss was a way of saying how much she needed the love of her father and how much she missed him. In a sense Ann's entire crisis brought a life-long pattern to a head, with many levels merging to force her, finally, to learn from the situation, rather than to continue to act out the dilemma. "Acting out" is jargon for behavior a therapist considers inappropriate. Therapists would prefer their clients talk out their conflicts, rather than do anything to express them.

Crises are learning opportunities in which a person can resolve conflicts which surface, as Ann's did, as a particular problem, but which reflect undercurrents long submerged outside of awareness. Therapy for Ann is a focusing on this learning process, indeed, on her entire growth process, and it offers her a more profound insight into contemporary social realities as well as how these realities affected her. Examples are the role of her father throughout her relationships with men, the sexist pattern Al acted out through his continual need to conquer and then reject women, and the role of lovers in contemporary society.

Bob is a thirty-two-year-old man. He has been married for five years and has one child. His wife, Betty, left him recently, accusing him of being insensitive and unresponsive to her needs. Bob sensed this was true, although it had not been his intention. He apologized profusely to Betty, promising to make changes in his life. Betty returned with the understanding that Bob had to change. How to change, how to become a more responsive person, what kind of person did Bob want himself to be, were the questions which led him into therapy. Betty refused to accompany him, correctly pointing out that Bob couldn't use psychotherapy as a means of working out his marriage as if that were his problem. He must first come to grips with his own identity, then see if marriage to Betty was a mutually acceptable means of working out what both of them wanted from their lives.

Bob's case is substantially different from Ann's. He is not coming to therapy devastated by a sense of impending catastrophe, although Betty may leave him again, but by a sense of his own limitations. Few men enter therapy (perhaps no more than 20 percent of clients are men); most resent the stigma of needing help. Bob's crisis had not precipitated an emotional collapse but a thorough reevaluation of his sense of self. Marriage had protected him from his own need to grow, offering a false sense of security. He had taken Betty for granted and had been lured into a complacency which proved illusionary when Betty left him. He had resisted her attempts to point out how limited their relationship was, how little he was doing with his life, how many demands he made on her for so little in return, by pointing out how few "problems" their marriage had. In terms of erupting conflicts, knock-down, drag-out fights, he was correct. But Betty's simmering discomfort, kept in check by her reasonableness, was just as real a problem as any which leads to overt suffering and battles.

Carla has a history of psychotherapy, even hospitalizations for "schizophrenic breakdowns." She had been seeing a therapist for over a year at the request of her mother. Gradually she began to deteriorate. Her attempts at establishing herself as an artist were interpreted by her therapist as an attempt to avoid her real responsibilities "as a woman"—to be married and have children. Yet relationships with men terrified her and rarely worked out. The therapist saw therapy as the solution to this problem. Carla began hearing voices, became unable to walk to work, and terrified her friends by recounting hallucinations. She would occasionally wake up screaming. Her roommate told her to tell her therapist, which she did. He suggested that she begin taking some tranquilizers or even a mild phenothiazine. She did and while her "symptoms" disappeared, she lost her job and began having promiscuous relationships with men. She didn't care about anything.

Carla's roommate, who had experiences with shrinks herself, kept pushing Carla to see someone else. She pointed out that Carla wasn't being helped. Carla rejected this advice and immediately stopped taking her medication to demonstrate how well she had herself under control. She found another job, established a close relationship with a man she met during a shopping trip, and told her therapist that he was correct: she didn't want to be an artist. Then she took an overdose of sleeping pills and woke up in the hospital.

In retrospect Carla realized her suicide attempt was a manufactured crisis designed to get her another therapist, any other therapist, who would support her in becoming the person she wanted to be. She could no longer conform to the oppressive demands of her therapist, however well meaning he was. Carla had attempted to conform completely, even to the extent of denying her most valued desire, to be an artist, because she was terrified of her hostility and the imagined impact rejection would have on her therapist, whom she liked very much. As with many women, she protected her therapist. He had viewed her attempts to be an artist, to commit her life to art, as symptomatic because he rejected the notion of a woman being anything other than a housewife and mother without being neurotic. From this point of view the behavior patterns resulting from the frustration of her desire were justification of his assumption she was neurotic instead of being perceived as a consequence of her oppression. Carla, under pressure, became confused, frightened that indeed, she may not *really* be an artist. She capitulated. This necessitated a rejection of herself. She tried to kill the unreal, oppressive personality others, including her therapist, wanted her to have, so she attacked her body, the symbol of her entrapment. It was as if she had to kill her body to escape and be truly free.

A second therapist, more aware of sexist biases in therapy, supported her reluctance to be married. He explained this pressure as a cultural bias of her previous therapist and declared there was no reason to suppose being married was necessarily any healthier for an individual than being single was. He also expressed interest in her art. She began to improve immediately and made plans to return to school to pursue this vocation.

Carla's crisis appears, on paper, relatively easy to resolve. The desires to pursue art and to be single were too easily passed off simply because her therapist disapproved. The extremely dependent relationship with her therapist and the unusual degree to which Carla would go to express her inner conflicts are problems which are likely rooted deeply in childhood and will express themselves in different forms throughout her life. Even seeing the therapist at a request from her mother seems to be a way of being a good, obedient child. The therapist, from this point of view, is an extension of her parents. His goals for her happened to coincide with those of Carla's parents. The therapist at the hospital proved helpful in resolving the crisis but did not probe into the complex background of the crisis.

Crises are often a helpful source of learning and provide the motivation for many people to get into therapy. They appear to be simple problems, once the person is in therapy, and they often are. Or they may reflect undercurrents which may take months, even years to reveal, explore, and resolve. Yet the crisis itself is usually over quickly, leaving the person feeling "helped" and anxious to terminate therapy. At this point there is no way to say such a decision is right or wrong, only that the use of therapy as a temporary means of bailing a person out has its own limits. People getting into therapy to alleviate distress and restore themselves to a functioning level are properly interested in terminating the relationship as soon as this is accomplished. Others may believe, "Now that I am here, let us continue until I have learned as much as this therapy relationship can teach me about myself and my world."

Occasionally people enter therapy for no other reason than that for a long time they have felt life has been meaningless and they want to find out if there is something they can do to feel more alive. They seem chronically depressed, flattened by the emptiness of their lives. These people are "normal," without "problems," and often live conventionally successful lives. But they are bored. By avoiding being alone, using stimulants and depressants, filling their lives with distractions like parties, television, movies, or compulsive work these people never seem to come to grips with the speed of their lives, their lack of reflection, or their aimlessness.

Dorothy is thirty-five. She graduated from college, earned a good living in advertising, met and married a successful executive, moved into a suburban neighborhood, had two children who are doing extremely well in school and in their relationships with other children. Dorothy left advertising when she became pregnant, and while her children were in school, she took tennis lessons, played bridge, shopped, and so forth. There were no areas of difficulty for her. She and her husband were good friends and lovers with no more than the usual conflicts. Yet one day she became interested in psychotherapy through a book she was reading. She spoke to friends who had been in therapy, talked it over with her husband, and one day (after a year of considering the possibility) she made an appointment.

It is not necessarily true that Dorothy had no problems but that they were not the kind we normally associate with psychotherapy. She had failed to realize her potentials. Her life did not require her to extend herself, to move beyond her limits and explore other areas of her personality or her role in society. In therapy, through the interpretation of dreams and in philosophical discussions about society, Dorothy began to want more from life. She gave up what now seemed trivial, self-indulgent activities like shopping and tennis and started working with her church group. Eventually she began to explore cooking, always an enjoyable activity for her, and created a catering service for her friends. The business expanded and became an important activity in her life. Through her church group she and her husband became aware of the spiritual dimension to life. They participated in study groups, retreats, even encounter groups. Eventually they learned group leadership skills and led these programs themselves.

Therapy offered Dorothy a formal means of reflecting upon her life and access to methods (dream interpretation, role playing, dialogue with other persons) which revealed aspects of her personality she had never known. Growth in therapy was not measured by relief of anguish or improved abilities to function properly. It was measured by her increasingly deep satisfaction in being who she is and in extending these dimensions of herself into the lives of other people.

Frank lived a mediocre life. He had minimal success in school, earned just enough to get by, had never attracted any woman strongly enough to be married (although he seemed to prefer bachelorhood). He read novels, went to movies, often spent evenings visiting close friends and playing cards. Psychotherapy for him was a means of talking to someone on a more intimate basis than he was used to. Frank's life was "o.k." He had no reason to change, he would say, but therapy offered him a chance to talk with someone.

Therapy is no magical road to happiness and self-fulfillment. For some people it is enough to have someone to talk to, for others it is a matter of life and death. In the last few years therapy has become an exciting method for learning. Not in the simple way Dorothy used therapy, but as a deliberate attempt to experiment with the limits of a person's consciousness, body, emotional life, and relationship to others and society. In this sense the therapy relationship offers a minimal structure in which a person takes whatever precautions can be taken before reaching out beyond his or her limits. To some this exploration of psychic boundaries has become the focus of their lives—a search for new, dramatic, provocative, and sometimes dangerous methods including drugs, communal living, meditation, travel, and so forth.

LSD therapy, bioenergetics, structual integration (Rolfing), gestalt therapy, primal scream therapy, nude marathons, and reevaluation counseling are examples of some of the better-known therapies, often promising dramatic "cures," touted by people who have been through the experience and proclaim the results. Therapies per se become idealized and are part of a curious process of search some people are going through. The other part is the increasingly large numbers of people who become "counselors" or "therapists" rather than clients or patients. These nonprofessionals are often outraged by conventional therapy and therapists (although their "training" often is having been through therapy themselves).

The deliberate search for authentic, freely chosen limits, the expansion of one's identity, leads people into therapeutic experiences as well as into therapy relationships. Therapeutic experiences include encounter and sensitivity groups, weekend retreats and conferences, residential programs like Esalen, and so on. The use of therapy for personal growth contrasts with the traditional pose of therapy as the treatment of mental illness. People seem to be saying that therapy (or its equivalent) must help them explore the mystery of being human in all its profundity. Therapy is being pushed out from its treatment aspect to its potential for exploration and liberation. It is imperative, then, for people getting into therapy to define their objectives and to seek therapists and methods which can help them realize these objectives.

Many therapists are reluctant to explain how the therapy experience may not or cannot be helpful. Thus, many people see therapy as omnipotent. Consequently, people assume that if they can only persuade their children, lovers, spouses to enter therapy, all will be well. One way a person can do this without resorting to force is to enter therapy himself or herself and then bring the person he or she sees as having a problem into therapy as well. The client in this situation often tries to manipulate the therapist into taking sides.

Mike and Kay had three children. The youngest seemed to be doing poorly in school, stayed up late at night, and fought with her parents all the time. Rather than bringing Jane into therapy as the "defined patient" and leaving her to be treated as many parents do, Mike and Kay understood that Jane's problems probably were related to what they were or were not doing. They assumed therapists were, or should be, experts on child raising.

The first session began with Mike and Kay outlining all of Jane's "problems," which amounted to not being or doing what her parents expected and demanded of her. Nothing she did do was wrong: she merely failed to live up to her parents' demands. She must be "disturbed" because of what she didn't do. Her parents pointed out that tests showed she could do better in school, and doctors had assured them nothing was physically wrong with her. Hence she must have a problem. What could Mike and Kay do about her problem? Surely they were deficient in some way.

In the course of therapy the parents gradually became aware that Jane did not experience her failings as problems. She experienced her parents' implicit rejection of her as a source of pain, and she was hurt that they thought she wasn't good enough. But she didn't want to do well in math and science. Through examining Mike and Kay's lives, their standards were put in perspective as extensions of what they had learned was best for them. Jane was seen as an extension of their needs, not as a person in her own right. Her strengths, including great ability in social relationships, were minimized or ignored. Jane was in serious difficulties because of her parents' well-meaning pressures on her to be different.

Eventually Mike and Kay realized they were seeking therapy for themselves, using Jane as camoflage. They were deeply insecure about their capacities as parents and held specific and demanding standards to ensure that their children did well. Kay, desiring to give all of herself to her children, felt completely demolished by any sign of failure in them, seeing it as failure in herself. This exclusive focus allowed her husband to appear supportive of her without any threat to his sense of power. When Kay collapsed he would enter the scene and demonstrate how needed he was as a father and husband. Jane was breaking down inside, her parents grew to understand, precisely because they were trying to be "good" parents, making excessive and unfair demands on her to meet needs the parents would not meet for themselves in a more direct and responsible manner.

Debbie and George dated for over two years before deciding to be married. Their marriage lasted for a year before both felt they needed therapy to "save" it. They came in expressly asking the therapist to help them resolve difficulties in their marriage. During the sessions, however, each would compete with the other for time to talk about himself or herself. The therapist asked if they would like separate sessions. During these sessions the therapist discovered that Debbie wanted to discuss issues like what she wanted to do with her life and whether or not to go to school instead of having children. The therapist responded, "It sounds like you find marriage oppressive."

George, on the other hand, told the therapist he had a lover. There was no doubt he did not intend to tell Debbie. Here was a case where both people found their marriage in trouble because each wanted to be single. The therapist brought them together and told them he felt they were both struggling to live like single people while being married. Six months later George and Debbie divorced amicably but continued to come to therapy individually. George stopped shortly after the divorce, evidently because he felt there was no further reason for him to be there.

Mike and Kay, George and Debbie, all entered therapy under an assumed purpose which disguised the real problem within their own lives. Mike and Kay had difficulties accepting their own value as parents and were driven to press Jane in order to find confirmation and affirmation from "doing everything we could for her." George and Debbie came ostensibly to save a marriage or, more accurately, to improve a marriage neither really wanted. In both cases therapy had first to uncover the real focus of the client's desire for therapy and then to explore this focus until the problems were perceived. At one point as the therapist suggested a shift in focus to Mike and Kay, Kay began to experience anxiety about therapy. She said they were in therapy to help Jane, not to deal with *her* problems. The therapist had been able to lay the groundwork for this change in focus well enough to let her see this really was needed. A false issue, then, may serve to bring people into therapy, but it can lead to their being unable to continue with therapy when their first line of defense (the focus on someone else) is challenged.

We can say as a general rule that when people enter therapy they can think of the experience as something for themselves, not as an altruistic act for someone else's benefit. It makes therapy more helpful to everyone involved if one is willing to see therapy as a personally helpful experience. By exploring our own involvement in other peoples' distress we will be able to help them (in both cases the express purpose was fulfilled, but in ways unanticipated by the parties involved). By denying our involvement, therapy is delayed and perhaps jeopardized.

When a person goes to a therapist it is unlikely he or she will be able to describe precisely his or her problems. Part of therapy is sorting out the many interrelated themes involved in any person's life and arriving at a mutually acceptable series of goals for the therapy process. It is possible to enter therapy with a clear idea of one's commitment to the process as treatment, crisis intervention, problem solving, or personal growth. Furthermore, to recognize full participation of anyone involved in the sessions will be necessary to any helpful resolution of the dilemmas facing everyone. It is deceptive to claim one's marriage or one's children are in themselves a problem without recognizing that to some extent, however unintentionally, one is participating in the problem.

By examining the circumstances surrounding the decision to get into therapy, you may be able to determine if it is a crisis, a long-standing personality problem, a desire to find companionship and support, a means of resolving conflicts one is having with others, and so forth. In other words, is the purpose a specific and immediate one? Or do you want to explore your life? Or is therapy specifically sought as part of an overall commitment to personal growth and the exploration of your limits? Getting into therapy means answering these questions as accurately and completely as possible.

2
What Is Psychotherapy?

People get into therapy for a variety of reasons. The idea that psychotherapy is just for people who are severely disturbed is outmoded. Indeed, evidence suggests that psychotherapy is least effective with people who are severely disturbed. A person can seek therapy for personality problems, because of a crisis in his or her life, for companionship, because he or she is bored and finds life less satisfying than he or she would like to, as a way of finding help for another person or relationship, or as a means of personal growth. And therapists accept virtually everyone who comes for help, regardless of his or her reasons. What is psychotherapy that it can be offered to so many different people with so many different needs and desires?

A literal translation of "psychotherapy" would be the offering of the service of healing powers and qualities to a person's soul or life. The more formal definition would be the treatment of illnesses or disabilities of the mind, which functions as the center of thought, feeling, and behavior. The difference is in how one views the problems facing our society.

The formal definition implies a restoration of functioning, helping the individual to return to a state of health equated with fulfilling socially defined, normatively evaluated tasks. Psychotherapists who share this perception of therapy tend to view normality as health: to the degree a person varies from social norms, he or she is neurotic, then psychotic. Some variance from literal obedience to norms is permitted by liberal therapists, even when the therapists finds the particular behavior personally distasteful. It is this sense of extremity itself that becomes an operational definition of a psychiatric problem. What is abnormal is neither necessarily harmful to anyone or pathological.

An example of this approach—defining problems by equating abnormal and socially unacceptable behavior with psychiatric disorders—is current controversy among psychiatrists about whether homosexuality is a psychiatric disorder. Doctors who argue that homosexuality per se is a disorder say that statistically homosexuality is abnormal. Certainly many fewer people are primarily homosexual in their preferences than are heterosexual. Arguing this position creates the question, when is a minority position ever *not* a psychiatric disorder, if we apply this principle? Furthermore, adherents to this position argue, homosexuality is unnatural. It prevents the individuals involved from having children. This argument is similar to the Catholic appeal to natural law in opposition to intercourse except when its intent is to create a child. Whether one agrees with the position that homosexuality is sick or not, one is making a moral, not a scientific argument. That much is clear, and trying to legitimize a moral position with the use of "scientific" nomenclature seems to obscure the nature of the judgment.

Many, if not most of the problems people experience in their lives are "minority" issues. One can imagine individuals who reject such contemporary goals of society as making money, achieving success, having a family, and being as lovable as possible or those who have distinctly unpopular ideas, such as living in a commune, being bisexual, and rebeling against social authorities. When the client who values alternatives confronts the therapist striving to adjust patients to conforming patterns of behavior, the results are often painful, definitely reducing the effectiveness of therapy. Clients can only react by rebelling against the therapist, a difficult act for most, or by capitulating. Clients who give in usually feel deep-seated resentment toward the therapist; they rarely feel satisfied by therapy even if they claim it was helpful. The influence of a therapist may be quite subtle and nonmalicious. While it may cloud the therapeutic issues, it may not destroy the therapy process completely, as in the following example.

Charlotte Buhler, in an article entitled "Psychotherapy and the Image of Man," repeats a conversation she had with a woman who is a homosexual. Buhler, in therapy, made "points . . . against homosexuality." "I always take a definite stand against homosexuality," she writes. At one point she asked the patient "whether maybe her homosexuality precluded this freedom ('A person should not feel forced to do certain things') because it prevented her by necessity from relating in a complete way to the other sex and because she would not have a family . . . it must leave your life incomplete."

Buhler's patient, Arlene, complained about the fact that being a homosexual was so unacceptable to society she had to limit herself to "mostly homosexual groups." She resented this curtailment of her freedom because, in effect, it made her dependent on her relationship with her lover. She could not choose to love Jenny; she needed to love Jenny. Buhler twists this to show that homosexuality is limiting, rather than that hostility toward homosexuality forces homosexuals to band together in small groups for support and affirmation, making them dependent on each other. It is difficult to believe that Buhler's attitude (she always lets "a patient feel that he does not lose my affection and willingness to work with him if he chooses to stay within the homosexual pattern") does not preclude the possibility that the patient must distort himself or herself to avoid losing the therapist's regard.

Indeed, Arlene at the end of treatment had to contend with the therapist's point of view—that homosexuality was neurotic and limiting in itself—and her own experience that "my feeling about men makes it [sexual relations] something repulsive which it is not with a woman." Instead of capitulating as some homosexuals have done in similar situations and trying to be heterosexual, Arlene accepted the idea of herself as neurotic and limited because she remained homosexual. In other words, she accepted a negative, invalidating concept of self in order to justify a preference which is not within her control. Buhler celebrates Arlene's adjustment because she felt "a *whole* person" despite her "neurotic limitations."

If she had not been so set against homosexuality, Buhler might have been able to reassure Arlene in her chosen life style, to help her trust the therapist enough to validate her own choices and preferences in therapy without compromising her identity, and to be able to make the choice to continue or not to continue the homosexual pattern without any penality or stigma. The point is not so much whether homosexuality is right or wrong, but whether therapists can be allowed to manipulate or influence clients in directions which are appropriate to the therapists' values, but not necessarily to the clients'. Anyone with a minority position a therapist finds unacceptable may find this position undermined by the implicit or explicit attitude of the therapist that the position is neurotic or psychotic.

It is true that for some people deviance from social norms is a painful, undesirable alienation. Their experiences have, to their way of thinking, unavoidably pushed them away from what they should be doing, should be feeling, should be thinking. These clients can and do feel better if the therapist helps them adjust to socially conventional forms to a greater degree than they are able to themselves. Adjustment and accomodation are not undesirable alternatives to offer a client in themselves, but the decision should be based on the client's values, needs, desires, and self-interest, not on the therapist's interpretation of socially acceptable behavior as the model of psychic health.

Capitulation is useless because it only increases the schism within the patient. After all, the patient has usually entered therapy because of the separation between his or her values and resulting personality and the norms of the society as represented by significant others and authority figures. Simply to accept the therapist's values is a sacrifice of integrity, however it may diminish anxiety and make the patient feel better for a short time. Recently a mother came to me and talked about her daughter's problem: the girl was "schizophrenic." I asked for specifics rather than descriptive (and judgmental) concepts.

Sally was living at home at the age of twenty-three. Her first therapist had ended therapy abruptly after four years when Sally suggested she was well enough to begin *thinking* about terminating. Being unprepared for completely severing the relationship, she reacted with a mild attempt at self-mutilation. The analyst did nothing, made no response. Sally, in desperation, tried to kill herself and had to be hospitalized. The analyst again did nothing. Sally needed to know she was loved and also needed to know the therapist would let her become independent. In effect, the therapist's coldness and lack of concern, after four years of therapy, was a severe punishment for her attempts to leave.

Her next therapist insisted the problem was the family's: they had to work it out together. Therefore, Sally could not leave home without the therapist and her parents interpreting it as a hostile act toward her parents and a way of undermining therapy (i.e. self destructive). After four more years the father, who wants his daughter to remain dependent on him, has managed to resist changing. Consequently Sally remains at home, unwilling, unable, or afraid to confront her therapist's values and insist on the right to her own life. She has surrendered her life to a continual and cyclical family pattern reinforced by the therapist's devotion to the idea of "family." The therapist moved to another city and the family remains essentially unchanged after Sally's eight years in therapy. She stays alone in her room when she is not in a day hospital program.

Between rebellion and capitulation the client can attempt some sort of compromise. Usually the client persists in doing what he or she really wants to do but accepts some sort of "punishment." Henry is an example. He found that his paranoia was obviously unacceptable to the therapist. His argument was that he was being persecuted by his neighbors, that no one liked him, that he could see no reason for their attitude. The therapist "knew" this could not be true: entire neighborhoods do not turn against someone, particularly for no reason. As it turned out this was the case, as a rumor persisted in Henry's neighborhood that he pushed drugs. Parents dragged children away from him as he walked home, openly whispered behind his back, threw things in his yard, and so forth. He had no way of knowing why they acted the way they did. Henry became convinced he was crazy and began to fulfill the stereotype of the schizophrenic. He insisted that everyone loved him, that his therapist in particular thought he was incredibly nice. Despite his incessant demands on everyone, unresponsiveness, and intense rages, he maintained this extremely unrealistic belief that he was universally loved. What he had done, of course, was to realize that sticking with his "paranoia" was crazy: therefore, to be sane, he had to become different. If sanity is defined by authority as craziness, then insanity becomes socially acceptable. The irony of the therapist's, position—that Henry was paranoid because that perspective confirmed his own world view that people give each other the benefit of the doubt and that Henry, if he was disliked, must be doing unacceptable things—was not lost on Henry.

Through his parody of the therapist Henry kept his senses while appearing to be mad. Often "schizophrenics" play the role of the fool, presenting a brutally honest portrayal of a situation, while qualifying this image as "crazy." Henry did not capitulate, although he did become what the therapist wanted him to be since he completely changed his perspective to do so, implying that his original paranoia was still, in his mind, not paranoia, but an accurate picture of his social environment. Even so, he did not have a strong sense of his own sanity and was willing to have the challenge to his perceptions and health upset his world entirely. Would he have become "schizophrenic" if his therapist had tested out his perceptions of Henry's neighborhood before drawing a conclusion about the accuracy of these perceptions? Perhaps he would, as his inherent sense of invalidity and self-doubt had obviously created an unstable sense of self. The therapist, however, played into Henry's uncertainty about himself.

Anyone getting into therapy should immediately discount the idea that therapists are able to be objective. What they say, what they don't say, when they say things, when they don't, in short, everything about the therapy session, including the decoration of the room, reflects the values of the therapist. The treatment model implies that psychotherapy is a science or, at least, implies the application of scientific methodology, that is, an objective, authoritative, factually based methodology which eliminates self-deception and collusion. This claim is untrue. Psychotherapy deals with the mind, an entirely hypothetical entity. Without being able to see and measure the mind, any statement about the mind cannot be proven true nor false. It can be believed or disputed, but never can it be fact. Psychotherapy is least helpful when confused with science and with the tremendous authority science and scientists have in our society. Ultimately a therapist's beliefs may be grounded in evidence, logic, and broad knowledge and, therefore, may be more likely to be useful than a client's; but the helpfulness of the values can only be discovered through experimentation, trial, and error. Clients must maintain a skeptical but fair attitude toward everything the therapist suggests explicitly or implicitly.

Therapy, whatever else it may be, is based on values and is heavily weighted in the direction of the therapist's values. These values being predominate, the client must avoid having to choose between rebellion, capitulation, or compromises which sacrifice integrity or health. Clients must identify the therapist's world view as quickly as possible. Any competent therapist will attempt to minimize the forcefulness his or her values may be expressed with simply because of the therapist's role and authority, but the client's best protection against emotional damage and unnecessary conflict with a therapist is to select a person or method which is largely congruent with the client's own value system.

That is not to say you should select a therapist who agrees with everything you do, say, feel, or think. Select one whose world view is open enough to encompass yours and offer you support for a wider number of alternatives and perspectives than you offer yourself. If you select a therapist who manifests social norms and assumes the purpose of therapy is to adjust and accomodate the patient to these norms, you may be urged to seek stability through conventional modalities. When a therapist has a limited world view, an essentially conservative one, the client with different values must fight his or her way out, compromise, or lose completely.

Several examples may clarify this point. Many married couples find their marriages are difficult and at times fear the hostilities or distances will lead to spiraling disruption and to divorce. Each person feels differently about the institutions of marriage and divorce, just as each therapist does. Linda and Mark were married two years, had one child, and fought constantly. They never reached any compromise; both said their marriage was hell. They had never thought about divorce because of its stigma. Their therapist told them they already were divorced, as they were completely apart in every way except where they lived. He suggested that they think about this and see what they came up with. Betty and Carl felt marriage was difficult but wanted to keep the relationship together, if they could. After a few months of therapy and considerable thought they told their therapist they wanted a divorce. The therapist said, "I don't counsel people for divorce, only for marriage," and refused to continue to see them. Patti and Eric found their therapist continually implying they should get a divorce. Patti found his disparagement of marriage particularly disturbing. They left therapy and tried for several months to work things out on their own. Eventually they tried another therapist who believed marriages can work out, even in difficult situations, if the couple is willing to work things out at some personal expense. Finally, Ricky and William took a troubled marriage to a therapist who never quite helped them out of their feeling that marriage was rewarding in many ways but sexually restrictive. The therapist felt this was one of the "penalties" or "sacrifices" one made for the benefits of marriage. Another therapist, less conventional, might have suggested they explore their fantasy of a sexually open marriage and see if this was something they wanted to try.

The importance of the therapist's values, of the therapist's idea of what is "healthy," is absolutely critical to any possibility that therapy will be helpful to the client. If Linda and Mark encountered a therapist who persisted in working things out until divorce eventually resolved the problem, Linda and Mark might have ended up divorced but, at the same time, felt they had failed. By recognizing that divorce was one possible solution, the therapist allowed them to realize their solution was divorce without a sense of having failed. Reflection allowed them to gain insight into their behavior and bring them both into touch with what they were feeling and doing. Betty and Carl went to another therapist but had to spend months working through their feelings of abandonment, rejection, and abuse by the first therapist. Patti and Eric encountered a liberal therapist who believed in divorce but didn't believe in marriage. Ricky and William's oppressive relationship persisted simply because their therapist couldn't conceive of any marriage being open enough to allow the couple to have sexual relations with others; therefore, he could not suggest ways the couple could safely explore this alternative before drawing conclusions.

If a limitation to the treatment model lies in the therapist's concept of what is healthy, that is, what the therapist's goals for the therapy relationship are, the client must insist that the therapist give the client a clear idea what the therapist's world view is. Each of the couples could have ensured that therapy would be helpful by finding therapists open to many different concepts of marriage, including marriage as a finite relationship which may be brought to an end without a sense of failure or inadequacy. Finding a therapist who is open to your limits but who cannot (or does not want to) extend your limits as you see them in beginning therapy may mean you are more secure while beginning therapy. After getting further into therapy, you may find you want to change or expand your original limits, but the therapist may not perceive these desires as positive since they go beyond his or her boundaries.

Conflict with a therapist is difficult because the client is in an inherently inferior position, having come to the therapist precisely because of the authority, knowledge, and skills associated with that role. Unfortunately and unintentionally, therapists may use their skills defensively, invalidating or obfuscating the client's need for change. A particularly effective weapon a therapist has is the use of interpretation. By calling into question the motivation of the client and his or her awareness of the motivation, the therapist may cause a client to become doubtful about what are, at best, intuitive responses to his or her own needs—growth. The therapist simply assumes such urges for experimentation outside the therapist's concept of acceptable and appropriate limits are destructive and unhealthy urges and treats them as such. Many people I know have had to get a considerable distance in time from their therapist's influence to realize that what they had wanted to try was indeed, for them, an important, self-fulfilling step.

The treatment model itself tends to reinforce conventional and conservative values. Psychotherapists involved in the treatment model are most often psychiatrists and psychologists, with much of their training, income, and prestige tied into the notion that psychotherapy is the "scientific" treatment of mental illness, itself a parallel to physical illness, according to this model. There is also the question of power. Psychiatrists involved in the treatment model can make diagnoses and categorize a person's behavior and state of being as an "illness," thereby causing society to discount the validity of the individual. They can also make dispositions, including commitment, drug therapy (often drugging the client to the point of insensibility and pliability), or simply hospitalization (with its attendant horrors of institutionalization and bureaucratic attacks upon dignity and sensibility). In other words, as R. D. Laing, Seymour Halleck, Thomas Szasz, Thomas Scheff, Erving Goffman, and others have pointed out, there is the strong element of self-interest involved in the support of the medical treatment model.

For people with conventional and socially conservative values, and this is not intended to be a negative statement, the treatment model reflects values which are entirely congruent with their own, and therapy under such conditions may be quite useful in helping them attain a "healthy" state of being. For people with values or needs which make conventional limitations and socially normative patterns oppressive or constricting, the treatment model will be emotionally damaging. The important element here is the need for prospective clients to understand their values and needs realistically enough to select or avoid any model which will threaten these values and needs or submerge them under false fronts.

An alternative model, which lies at the other end of a broad and varied spectrum from the treatment model, is based on the concept of psychotherapy as a healing process for the mind, the soul, the person's life. For this model existence is problematic. Anyone can have "problems in living" which therapy can be helpful in exploring and perhaps resolving. Normality is treated with skepticism: some have gone so far as to suggest that being "normal" in an insane society is insanity. Certainly what many consider to be a negative and highly undesirable state of mind—schizophrenia—is, for some adherents to this model, an understandable, if not entirely acceptable, response to pathological environments.

The importance of the healing model is the broad philosophical and humanistic base behind it. A person is seen as having potentialities and dimensions that society, if it does not actively repress, certainly provides a poor environment for exploring, reflecting upon, and integrating into the person's life. Abraham Maslow made a powerful impact when he disclaimed the emphasis on pathology by stating that psychologists need to understand what is healthy. He went further than socially normative standards to define "healthy" and found evidence to support the contention that healthy people are capable of having "peak experiences," intense growth. Rather than seeking stability and homeostasis, in this view, healthy people change and enjoy the process of changing, despite the anxiety and frustration which often accompany change.

The healing model, focused on personal change and growth and ultimately on social change, implies people are all basically healthy. Society corrupts or oppresses each individual, turning everyone into a fragmented, alienated, incomplete person: only it affects some more than others. As a healing relationship psychotherapy is the exploration of the outer limits of the individual, assuming, therefore, an inner core or center of strength.

Just as the treatment model is restrictive when applied to people who do not want to be "normal" in every conventional nuance of the word but want to change themselves in order to fulfill their needs, even at the expense of being "unconventional" in attitude, emotions, or lifestyle, the healing model is disasterous for people who are disturbed and need treatment. Here is the complex but critical crux of the issue. In order to help people grow, that is, experiment, risk, and test boundaries, psychotherapists and therapies must be flexible and at times ambiguous or even chaotic about boundaries. Treatment-oriented therapists are highly structured and formal. (Remember the continuum and the fact we are discussing the poles: there are in reality many different interpretations and overlaps between these two models. This structure, formality, and stability or reliability is important in working with highly disturbed people. Yet these same aspects become restrictive and oppressive when one is (or becomes) "centered." Being centered means being in touch with one's feelings, values, priorities, and immediate experiences.

Existentialism suggests that living is a problematic condition: when we subject society to a trenchant analysis, we see the extent to which people suffer anxiety, alienation, fragmentation, unfulfilled potential. Society, if not actually repressive, is at least unresponsive to and unsupportive of changes in people or institutions that reflect needs and aspirations instead of power and profit. Consequently people need helping relationships to restore them to integrated, functioning wholes. From this point of view, normality, to the extent it reflects stability, resistance to change, the status quo, may be seen as in itself a form of mental illness. In a society where institutions (school, marriage, the family, business) are hostile to human sensibilities and needs and where simply existing subjects people to brutalizing, degrading, hostile, competitive experiences, common sense indicates that anyone will need a helping relationship aimed at supporting growth and actualizing potentials.

This world view is the direct opposite of the world view behind the treatment model, that society expresses the means of fulfilling people and that accomodation to society is the road to health and well-being. Thus it is logical to expect that the healing of the soul model has a different perspective on what constitutes psychotherapy and health. And it does. Rather than seeing people with problems as "sick," that is as suffering from an inner source of distress and unbalance, the relationships between people are considered the root of personality problems and difficulties in living. In other words, personality is the sum total of interpersonal experiences. To the extent an individual has had responsive, tender, empathetic, supportive relationships, that person will have been able to grow and to become the expression of his or her potentials. Anxiety-filled relationships marked by manipulative, controlling, and punitive characteristics, depriving the individual of an environment conducive to growth, will create a person with a suspicious attitude toward others, defense systems against anxiety which will distort and disrupt ongoing relationships (and paradoxically avoid learning), and patterns of interacting which preclude pleasure, intimacy, and satisfaction of needs.

In other words, the healing model is interpersonal or interactional. What happens between people is emphasized. Inner states of thought (dreams, fantasies, ideas, interpretations of reality, philosophies), emotions (reflected in the body, in expression, symbolically through creativity), and activities (communication, lifestyle, political activities, sexuality) are not evaluated against a series of normative standards, but by the individual's desires, needs, and aspirations. The healing process seeks to explore, experiment with, understand, and finally integrate the intrapsychic processes of being with interpersonal relationships within the framework of the individual's entire life.

The treatment model is often restrictive and oppressive when a person is capable of risk taking and desires experimentation. The growth model is often destructive to those people who are extremely disturbed. This is an ironic and unfortunate aspect of the growing disparity between these two methods and the resulting confusion which exists. The strength of the treatment model lies in its tendency to be a structured, formal, even impersonal approach to the individual, although a genuinely caring one. To someone who is terrified, filled with visions of self-mutilation and destruction or urges to destroy and mutilate others, unable to distinguish the self from others, real messages from delusions, enemies from sources of help, the treatment model (even the phenothiazines) is clearly helpful. If the individual does not cease to be mad, at least he or she may cease to be in extreme psychic pain and anguish. People on the verge of extreme states of consciousness (and the corresponding loss of discriminatory ability, hence control or influence over the state) we consider psychosis are not helped by the often confused, ambiguous, unreliable, inconsistent, and sometimes threatening lack of boundaries and structure characteristic of the humanistic approach to therapy. Yet it is precisely the flexibility, even the lack of structure and limits which is a strength of the healing model, for this allows people to explore areas which are generally ignored, restricted, or repressed.

Bonnie was a timid individual who thrust herself into situations because she trusted others to take care of her. Inside she was frightened, outside eager to please, to be liked, to try anything other people were involved in. For many years Bonnie had fought back a desire to be loved by anyone, believing she was unlovable. Of course she failed, but not completely. She succeeded to the extent that she approached any offer of love or caring believing it would prove unreal. What she wanted was a complete union with another person. She would offer such a lover anything, should he prove trustworthy, capable of withstanding such a loathesome person as herself. Bonnie was asked to go to an encounter group by a friend.

The group met each week for two hours. Eventually Bonnie, impressed by the charisma of the leader (a man who showed compassion, tenderness, and the ability to challenge people), opened up her feelings of helplessness and rage. Yet the group still offered support, even embraces and caresses. For the first time in her life Bonnie felt complete and fulfilled. Then the group ended. Bonnie made a serious attempt on her own life, was rushed to a hospital, and tried once more, in an ambulance on the way to a mental hospital.

Bonnie interpreted the end of the encounter group as a personal rejection, an abandonment which left her without defenses against her self-hate, loneliness, and deep-seated conviction that without love and acceptance her life was living death. Of course such extremely distorted perceptions are rare, but when the encounter groups began and leaders naïvely assumed all the members could take care of themselves (unless their behavior in the group indicated otherwise), a small percentage of participants did try suicide or became more overtly disturbed when the groups ended. Bonnie thrived in the group and probably appeared to be an ideal group participant. Her "madness" fed upon the end of the group experience, not the content of it.

Bonnie improved enough to return to living on her own over the following two years. She saw a staid, conventional therapist, following a strictly medical-treatment model all the way. Yet the structure, the lack of demands, the sense of unlimited time (despite the finite session which ended all too soon, she knew she had years to recover), and the extremely consistent behavior of her therapist helped. She learned a modicum of trust in other people and in her abilities to influence her own life. A friend of mine once said that a therapist, to be successful with schizophrenics, must have infinite patience and tolerance for boredom. Such an approach to a centered person, capable and desirous of peak experiences, would be stultifying and oppressive, but such is the paradox of psychotherapy.

We can say, then, that psychotherapy is a helping relationship, but one which, in order to be utilized, must be understood more fully. The critical difference among approaches to psychotherapy is in the world views of the therapists. The world view which conforms most thoroughly to conventional middle-class values (work, family, nothing in excess, obedience to authority) is the medical-treatment model. This model seeks to apply therapy to problems characterized by the degree to which the individual is unable to accept or function in terms of socially acceptable limits and expectations as interpreted by authority figures, particularly the therapist. The world view which challenges the prescribed standards of the society (whether a particular area like the body, sexuality, emotions or in general like the radical therapists' critique of society and social definitions of the person) is represented by the healing model, understood in the most symbolic sense of making whole a person's life and soul—revitalizing the human spirit. Within these two poles are many approaches to problems which have slightly different interpretations of what is acceptable, healthy, or a worthy goal for a client.

Getting into therapy means searching for the therapist and approach that is close enough to your own world view and value system as not to be threatening or cause you to feel competitive or defensive, yet broad enough to extend beyond your pretherapy boundaries so there will be room to change. Specific guidelines for choosing an appropiate therapist will be discussed in a later chapter.

3
The Uses of Therapy

Between the broad definitions of therapy as a treatment process oriented toward helping people adjust and conform to socially normative lifestyles with a minimal amount of deviance and therapy as a growth process helping people to explore their personalities and potentials, therapy has a variety of purposes or uses.

A common use is to explore the issues bringing the person into therapy in the first place. Hardly anyone finds that the reasons he or she entered psychotherapy are the ones he or she remains in therapy to deal with. By discussing the "precipitating event" or crisis which motivated the person to seek help, a client is able to explore the complexity of issues underlying his or her immediate dilemma. Eventually these issues become dominated by recurring themes, themes which can be traced back to early childhood and sometimes into the lives of one's parents and grandparents.

Andre sought out therapy because he was unhappy at home. Since he had turned twenty-one, he felt it was time he became independent, yet he was depressed, lacked the initiative to move out of his home, and assumed he had "problems." During the first session he insisted there was nothing his parents were doing to keep him home, despite his statement that they didn't charge him any rent or board. He admitted that his father had bought him a color television for his room. The therapist suggested that these were incentives to remain at home and be taken care of, rather than incentives to move out on his own. Andre admitted this was true but added that his parents probably didn't realize this.

In the second session the therapist discovered that the household included Andre's paternal grandparents. Indeed, the grandfather, who kept referring to Andre as a "good son," encouraged Andre's father to support Andre: "He's got his whole life to be on his own, there's no hurry about him getting out." Andre was surprised when the therapist suggested that his grandfather seemed to be influencing his father and him to a considerable extent. It was the key insight. He began listing all the decisions his grandfather made for his father and described how dependent his father was on the grandfather. The therapist asked what seemed to lead to his father to be dependent on the grandfather. Andre didn't know.

The third session began with Andre making a joke that since they were spending so much time in therapy discussing his grandfather, the therapist should invite the grandfather to attend. The therapist responded seriously to this casual statement by saying, "Yes, it does look like your grandfather's attempts to control everyone are causing your difficulties in your attempt to become independent. I can imagine you living with your children in your father's home." Andre denied he would ever do this but admitted that unless he left home that was an idle boast. Yet he lacked the energy. Rather than perceiving this as a symptom of neurosis (and therefore a problem which must be resolved within Andre's consciousness) the therapist suggested that the lack of energy and initiative resulted from Andre's awareness of how difficult it would be to confront both his parents and his grandfather about his desire to break away from their attempts to control his life and keep him dependent. This focused Andre on the problems between his parents and himself, rather than leading him into what his problem was. He began to see that his situation was not the result of just his "problems" but was contributed to by the needs and demands of his parents and grandparents.

Andre accepted the idea of his dilemma as an "understandable" response, but certainly not the best one, to demands placed upon him in subtle and not so subtle ways. Such a definition didn't immediately resolve the dilemma, of course, but it gave Andre a new direction to pursue in therapy. At this time he might have renegotiated the therapy contract to one where the therapist would help him deal with his relationships with his parents and grandparents, rather than help him explore his vague and unfocused feelings.

Restating the goals of the therapy is done to accomplish three things. The first is to clarify how the therapy relationship has accomplished Andre's original purpose: to sort through and define his feelings of dis-ease and having "problems." The second is to give Andre the chance to focus more directly on the issue, rather than to allow him the opportunity of avoiding this issue by searching for other "problems." The third is to decide on the most practical approach, which in this case may be to involve the entire family network in therapy, rather than just Andre. They may be uncooperative, but it would facilitate the therapist's attempt to elucidate the complex dependency relationships.

Once therapy resolves the focal conflict, in this case Andre's general sense that something was wrong with him because he was still living at home, had no energy, and was depressed a lot, the particular therapy relationship may become meaningless. This may happen whenever a new level is reached. There are many reasons for this, and because it is important to understand this phenomenon, it would be wise to consider the circumstances behind such a change before continuing to describe other uses of psychotherapy besides clarifying conflicts.

In Andre's case the new focus of therapy raises a particularly difficult question: is the therapist, who has been helpful up to this point, skilled enough to handle the new direction or method the situation indicates? The therapist may choose to continue seeing Andre alone, not because it is the most helpful method for dealing with family issues but because the therapist lacks the skills and confidence to deal with the entire family. Such a problem is difficult for many clients to accept. The natural inclination is for clients to believe or want to believe in their therapists, despite any and all evidence their minds give them that such a belief is unwarranted or, at least, should be tempered with skepticism.

In situations where the therapist is fully willing and able to continue to work with the client on a new level or dimension, the client may be unwilling to continue. This desire to leave or, at least, to stop working in therapy is usually the client feeling unmotivated to continue, is the result of a variety of things. The client often has resolved the initial and relatively superficial problems which brought him or her into therapy, a fact which relieves some of the anxiety and leaves him or her relatively comfortable. And, at the same time, the client may be aware of what appear to be endless, insurmountable problems ahead. A client facing such problems often wants to avoid them, which means avoiding or ending therapy. The client complains the therapist has either "solved" the problem, or "made things worse," shifting the responsibility for his or her antipathy toward continuing therapy onto the therapist.

Because the therapist has been helpful or, at least, has tried to be helpful, clients often continue in therapy to avoid hurting the therapist's feelings. They are reluctant to say that therapy has ceased to work for them, possibly because they sense that the underlying problems or personality traits which create problems are essentially untouched. Yet eventually the client eases out of therapy, possibly by missing sessions, congratulating the therapist on how helpful he or she has been but mentioning how little else needs to be done.

Regardless of the reasons, the client experiences the therapy relationship as over, while he or she still has unfinished business. An ex-client syndrome is beginning to be noticeable. This brings us to another reason for going into therapy: to continue working on basic life themes which have been revealed to some extent in previous efforts in therapy but continue to be unresolved to some problematic degree for the individual. The person is not completely integrated yet has done some real changing.

Andre did find his therapist reluctant to continue working with him if that meant calling in the parents and grandparents. So he continued with the therapist on a one-to-one basis for a six-month period. During this time he found out a great deal about himself, gained some self-confidence, and in many ways became more independent. But he still remained at home. The therapist's method, to analyze the collusive, reinforcing patterns of interactions a client is stuck in, had helped Andre understand how his dependency was not entirely his problem, but it had been unable to create the spark necessary for Andre to make a significant change. After six months Andre dropped out of therapy, explaining that he just had to do things on his own. He couldn't continue depending on the therapist.

After a few months of being out of therapy, Andre heard of a woman who was particularly helpful in working with families. He persuaded his mother and father to attend a session with him, pointing out that there must be something wrong with the family since they were all depressed to some extent. The mother explained to the family therapist that she was concerned because Andre was still living at home. The father said he thought there was plenty of time for Andre to work that out. Andre felt a sudden surge of hostility and contempt for his father, remembering his previous therapist pointing out how Andre's father was still dependent on *his* father. "Oh yeah! What about you?" Andre screamed. "You still cling to your old man, doing everything the way he tells you to do it."

Andre's father expressed deep hurt, and his face showed considerable pain at this outburst. He admitted he was very close to his own father and did what he did because he loved him. This implied that Andre's desire to break away from his father was equivalent to not loving him. The therapist pointed this out and focused in the following sessions on how confused the family was about love, natural processes of growth and maturation, and the role of parents in supporting children to "leave the nest." Andre's mother finally insisted that Andre leave and that his father had no business holding him back. Andre, still fundamentally dependent on his parents, needed to be told to leave in order to do so. Paradoxically, he could not have left until his parents gave him permission. The therapist did not point this out because she felt the important thing was for Andre to make a move away from his parents, not to be fully confronted with the depth of his dependency needs.

Andre was asked by the family therapist at the conclusion of the treatment (the family developed to a more conventional form: father and mother at home, son out on his own, father beginning to move out from under the domination of his father—neither grandparents would come into therapy) if he wanted to continue therapy in a group. Andre felt he needed some support, at least for a while, to be on his own.

Therapy can serve the purpose of supporting people through major transitions during their lives. This is particularly true of group situations. Young people emerging into adolescence or from adolescence into independence, couples getting married, married people in the process of divorce, men or women changing lifestyles (communes, particularly during the first two years, often use therapists to help them sort out the changes they must make to adapt to a new, radically different lifestyle) are all examples of transitions through which many people need support. Usually people develop support networks, "friendships," which help them weather major crises in their lives. When no network exists or the existing network is not helpful, participation in therapy or groups is a substitute.

Andre found his group challenged his need for approval and permission from the group leader. Through this experience Andre became more aware of the range of his dependency. At first he thought his dependency on his parents was an isolated phenomenon, and if he were to separate from them, he would no longer be dependent. Now he realized he had been trying to have a similar relationship with the group leader. In addition, through the group Andre learned that he was likable and, although he was relatively immature for his age, that there were activities in his city where he could find peers. The group offered resources—suggestions, encouragement, criticism, friendship, even occasional fighting—the therapist alone could not offer. Andre found in the structured and relatively managed group experience that he was not demolished by someone's anger toward him, that he could argue with people without losing their friendship, and, finally, that they would support his moving beyond even the group.

Sometimes people seek therapy for a particular problem, and the only thing they want or will accept as therapy is the removal of the problem. Often this problem is a sign of deeper levels of conflict and unresolved themes, but the client is not interested. A method which has proven effective in "symptom removal" is behavior modification. Through such an experience a client can work on smoking, drinking, masturbation, homosexuality, obsessive-compulsive rituals, and so forth. Generally therapy has not proven to be as helpful in such situations as peer groups like Alcoholics Anonymous or behavioral modification approaches. Residential treatment programs, whether houses for drug addicts or institutional settings for disturbed or delinquent children, generally offer a structured milieu which, over time, offers a possibility that the individual will emerge without continuing with the "symptom" which brought him or her into the program.

Particular symptoms are often extremely difficult to work with, and evidence suggests that even the approaches of residential, peer group, or behavioral modification programs are not entirely effective. Much depends on the cooperation of the clients. Without a firm resolve to eliminate the "symptomatic behavior" from their lives and willingness to undergo the consequently drastic reshaping of their entire personalities by the "program" which is often necessary, the individuals will defeat and subvert every effort. Indeed, the inclination to do so is so strongly evident in many of these clients that only a group of people who have been through the games and recognize manipulation and deceit are able to counteract the games long enough to allow the clients to come to decisions to rid themselves of the patterns they are caught up in.

Exploring specific areas of experience, for example, dreams, often brings people into therapy. They want to understand more of an area of their lives and to integrate this material into their ongoing selves. Dreams are a fascinating area of human experience. People have always looked to dreams as a way of opening up the mysteries of human experiences and the future. Freud developed an approach to dreams which allows people to understand more about the themes and dynamics of their unconscious. Jung's approach to dreams not only helps the individual understand the literal message of a dream, but ties this meaning into the rich history of myth, other cultures, and a concept of consciousness expanded over Freud's. Perls, using the techniques developed in psychodrama, has approached dreams as fragments of the personality. By identifying with each fragment one not only begins to understand the meaning of dreams, one is able to integrate the fragments into one's personality.

By entering therapy-as-an-exploration-of-dreams the client is selecting a particular modality or approach to understanding himself or herself. Occasionally a therapist will suggest exploring dreams as the basic method for understanding and exploring the self or use dreams as one of several approaches. The problem of selecting one therapist or one approach is the rarity of finding a therapist who is experienced and multiskilled enough to develop all levels of experience. Dreams are one way of exploring intrapsychic levels, just as they may be incorporated in a more complete analysis of the mind or self based on Freudian or Jungian guidelines. By stressing one dimension of experience, however, the threads or themes of each problematic theme which stretch into other levels are either incompletely resolved or ignored.

Another example of a specific area of experience is structural integration, or Rolfing (named after Ida Rolf, its discoverer), which involves the realignment of the muscles and bones by a massage which separates fascia, or connective tissues that have grown together because of poor posture or repressed tension. Theoretically, chronic poor posture or the tightening of muscles as a result of repressed emotions causes the fascia to stick together. Rolfing, by separating the fascia, allows the muscles and skeletal structure to flow in a natural, unrestrictive way. The method requires ten sessions, and for some people it can be quite painful. However, despite the lack of scientific research on the positive (or negative) effects of Rolfing, people seem to be fascinated with the idea. Certain immediate visible effects, such as improved posture, more flexible limbs, and filled-out muscular shapes, support the largely intuitive judgments of people who seek Rolfing that the changes are desirable. People sense they are out of touch with their bodies and desire to be more fully physical, healthy, and natural than modern life influences us to be. The return to the body is evident in the reviving interest in massage, bioenergetics (largely a series of physical exercises which are connected with repressed emotions), nutrition, exercise, and health clubs.

A third example is the interest of married couples in discovering new areas of interest, new intensities of involvement, in their marriages by attending sexual therapy together, weekends in which a combination of intensive dialogues, group discussions, lectures, and series of questions raise issues concerning their relationships.Couples also enter standard therapy relationships, ostensibly to deal with "problems" but more to improve the overall quality of the relationship.

Sometimes people live extremely painful, empty lives, continually involved in situations which drain them of energy and perpetuate their loneliness, self-hate, and patterns of interactions which alienate or hurt others. They are unable to view therapy as a means of expanding their limits; they want relief from their anguish. They seek therapy as a means of resolving their problems in living and are committed to extensive changes in their personalities.

Therapy can, with a properly committed, sincere client and a therapist who is capable of sustained therapeutic relationships, help a person undergo the changes necessary to improve the overall quality of his or her life and to develop a personality and way of relating to people which gives satisfaction. Some people who are deeply disturbed and have had childhoods without much happiness and tenderness are unable to continue with any relationship, even therapy, because they develop intense fears of being destroyed by the intimacy. They often go from therapist to therapist, waiting until the relationship gets to the point where they can no longer handle it, then leaving.

A common but largely false assumption about psychotherapy is that it is primarily for people who are neurotic or psychotic. This becomes more untrue all the time as the need for psychotherapy becomes felt by larger numbers of people and therapists expand their own understanding of the therapeutic relationship. Neurotic behavior has become so common it is difficult to draw distinctions between people who are idiosyncratic, contradictory, or unhappy and those who are "disturbed." Everyday life is so problematic, confusing, and unsatisfying, relationships so estranged, that people who are doing well, enjoying life, and finding their activities meaningful are "abnormal."

In this context therapy as a form of treatment has been modified to be therapy as a form of problem solving. Problem solving takes two forms: in-depth long-term therapy aimed at dealing with a problem and crisis intervention. Long-term therapy is not long compared with classical analysis. It may last between six months and a year, while analysis may last two or more years when the goal is personality change. The focus in long-term therapy may be on a marriage, a problem child, severe depression (possibly associated with a suicide), functional problems (such as inability to hold a job, failure in school, family problems), or personality problems which are associated with inadequate maturation as opposed to environmentally induced, life-long disorders (problems in relating to the opposite sex, sexuality, underlying convictions of being a failure, constant fears, and so on).

Crisis intervention is slightly more common than problem-solving therapy. Here therapy is used by the client as a specific solution to a major conflict. The crisis is usually the culmination of many unresolved themes in a person's life surfacing symbolically as a result of some specific, unexpected, unwanted change. The therapy relationship begins when the client comes to the therapist. By delineating the themes which created the crisis, the therapist is able to defuse the situation while providing the client with a growth experience.

Gerri slit her wrists and was brought to the hospital. The therapist uncovered the fact that her boyfriend had left her the day before. She had become depressed, figured life wasn't worth living, and tried to kill herself. The attempt was dramatic but not serious enough to cause Gerri any real damage. She had invested much emotion in her relationship and felt completely rejected, worthless, and unlovable as a result of the break-up. This was not an unusual crisis for a girl between the ages of fourteen and sixteen, the therapist felt, and after making sure she felt people did care for her ("My parents certainly made a fuss, didn't they?") the therapist sent her home.

To keep her longer or to involve her in therapy would have been an overresponse. Had the attempt been made because of family problems or situations which were likely to reoccur, short-or long-term problem-solving therapy might have been indicated. Making more from what she had done than what she felt the action indicated (a concrete example of her loss) would have been an intrusion into her life which she would not have welcomed. The therapist told the parents to be supportive, that is, not to make her feel badly for the way she acted. There were signs that Gerri needed her parents to reaffirm their love, but their solicitous attentions and obvious concern made it evident she was going to receive the affirmation of her value she needed. If Gerri seemed depressed again, the parents were to call the hospital.

Debbie is ten years old. Her father died suddenly, and Debbie became morose, stopped eating, and appeared confused and disoriented. The first day her mother brought her to the therapist she appeared slightly cheered. The therapist asked to speak to her alone. She cried when the therapist spoke to her of her father's death. In the second visit she still seemed to be sad. The therapist suspected there was more to her depression than the loss of her father. During the session he discovered that she feared her mother would leave her and never come back.

Through discussions of this issue among Debbie, her mother, and the therapist, the fear became manageable. Over a relatively brief period of time Debbie's moods improved, and the therapy was terminated. Many times dealing with a crisis is not straightforward. For example, a mother brought her son into therapy because he was misbehaving in school. During the interviews the mother made it very clear she had felt inadequate and powerless as a mother ever since her husband died several years before. The therapy was continued for six months working with the mother's unresolved grief, her dependency needs, and the messages she continually gave to the boy that he should become a replacement in some ways for his father.

Therapy may be used, then, as a means of defining problems, conflict resolution or problem solving, crisis intervention, personal growth experience, long-term analysis focusing on personality change, work with specific problems or illnesses like alcoholism, and the exploration of specific areas of human experience. The purpose of therapy is entirely defined by the needs of the client modified by the interventions and interpretations of the issues by the therapist. It is a mutual decision, in other words. Clients going into therapy must not only choose therapists based on the basic approach to therapy, but must then also work toward defining, within those parameters, the uses of the therapy.

The function of therapy, whether it is problem solving, personal growth, or crisis intervention, is simply the purpose the client uses the therapy to accomplish. To the extent the therapist is helpful in defining the most reasonable use for therapy, it is a mutual decision. Sometimes it may happen that the therapist is unable or unwilling to define the function of therapy, that is, what is accomplished, in a way which matches the needs and desires of the client. The best way a client has of avoiding this disparity of interests is to create an agreement with the therapist as to what the initial focus of therapy will be, renegotiating the contract as different levels or dimensions surface in the relationship.

Only by having a clear, explicit, mutual agreement as to the purpose of a segment of therapy or the entire relationship, can there be supportive efforts by both therapist and client toward an end which is acceptable to the client. A therapist working at cross purposes with a client, on issues which are not relevant to the client's central concerns, or through methods which are inappropriate to the issues is not only being unhelpful, but he or she may actually create emotional damage. Yet without a reasonably clear picture of what uses the therapy is being put to, the client has no way to anticipate or perceive these disparities until the discomfort becomes too intense to continue or a considerable time has elapsed after terminating and the expected "help" is absent.

What kind of psychotherapy should one seek? Personal growth oriented or treatment? In therapy how should one use the experience? To clarify problems? To deal with crises? To resolve difficult problematic situations? To explore areas of experience or personality? To deal with concrete problems like smoking or alcoholism? As a means of coping with neurotic or psychotic disorders?

These questions do not have to be answered before beginning therapy, but the sooner and more honestly they are answered, the more positive and helpful psychotherapy will be. Because of beliefs in the therapist clients are often reluctant to terminate therapy or to go on in therapy with another therapist. Yet the client pays for therapy and in a way shares the work load (therapy is not done for you, but with you) equally with the therapist. If the therapist has been helpful, fine, but the client owes the therapist nothing. And if therapy has not been helpful, prolonging the experience will not change this. Finally, without answering these questions the client cannot evaluate therapy or make trustworthy decisions about what is helpful or harmful. Indeed, neither can the therapist.

4
Choosing a Therapist

The choice of a therapist is the most critical decision involved in entering a therapy relationship, and it is also the most difficult. If the emotional and intellectual distance between therapist and client is too great, the alienation will damage the client emotionally and psychically. This damage may not appear immediately. Sometimes clients realize the extent to which they have subjugated their values to their therapists' only after they have terminated the relationship and gained some distance. The relationship between client and therapist is the critical factor in determining whether or not therapy will be helpful. Beyond the many factors which complicate the decision personally, some clinics and agencies make matters worse by assigning clients to therapists without regard for the client's judgment, needs, or desires. It is almost impossible for most clients to tell their therapists they want to change therapists. Despite the difficulties involved, not the least of which is the tendency on the part of many clients to have others make the complicated decisions in their lives for them, it is imperative that individual clients make this decision to the best of their abilities.

Obviously the first decision involved should be made before finding therapists to choose from. First, decide what kind of issues are to be the basis for psychotherapy. That is, do you want crisis intervention, family or marital counseling, personality-oriented therapy, or simply an exploration of the issues and themes involved in the situation and experiences you are coping with at the time you enter therapy. Second, determine what approach to psychotherapy you want to take. Do you see therapy as a form of treatment or as an exploration of the dilemmas involved in personal growth? Both approaches deal with problems, as we have seen, but from entirely different perspectives.

On the basis of these two areas of consideration, you are ready to look for a particular therapist. One may begin by assuming that therapists in private practice are generalists, meeting the needs of whatever clients come to them and are most often treatment-oriented unless they specify otherwise. The combination of eclectic problem-solving and treatment approaches is practically an economic necessity for anyone who wants to thrive in private practice. Therapists who strive to help the person grow (often referring to themselves as humanists) tend to work in centers (therapy, counseling, or personal growth programs). Programs which refer to themselves as clinics, agencies, or institutions are usually treatment-oriented but may be specifically for family problems, crisis intervention, or children. Large institutions take people who are in extreme states of consciousness and always stress adjustment to socially acceptable norms.

These generalizations imply there are clear differences, but don't be deceived. Individuals work where they can find jobs, and it is entirely possible to find a personal growth-oriented therapist in a treatment-oriented institution, although it is less likely to find a treatment-oriented therapist in a personal growth program. They are just guidelines to help narrow down the possibilities. My own bias is toward therapists who see psychotherapy as a relationship seeking to help the individual realize himself or herself on all levels, including political ones. However, anyone who wants to (and basically does) subscribe to the traditional values of the society or who simply wants problems resolved just enough so the anguish goes away may find him or herself in a unhappy situation with a therapist who thinks about problems differently. Furthermore, it is possible (say by choosing a psychoanalyst) to find essentially conservative and orthodox therapists who stress the analysis of the entire personality from childhood on, a process which may be growth producing and certainly is lengthy. The important thing is to decide what you want.

Choosing an agency is not equivalent to choosing a therapist. Although most agencies tend to be bureaucratic and process clients according to which therapists have "room," clients may and should protest this. Consider the therapist your employee, because you do pay for his or her time. Select the best, and don't let the awesome "authority" of an institution or a hierarchy deter you from making your own choice. Because therapy depends on the client-therapist relationship being trusting, open, intimate, safe, and mutually challenging (you offer the therapist a unique person to work with, while the therapist offers you different—and often difficult to accept and integrate—perspectives on yourself), finding out that you don't like, trust, feel safe with, or accept as a person your therapist long after the relationship is underway is a waste of time, energy, money, and morale.

Investigate the therapist. One way to do this is by talking to the therapists's other clients. The therapist can ask current clients if they will call you at your home (referring to you by your first name or even a code name, if you prefer to remain anonymous—they can remain anonymous as well) and talk to you about how they find therapy with this particular therapist. It is simpler, of course, if you know some friends who have been to this therapist and who can tell you something about the way he or she works or about him or her as a person. Try to talk to more than one person, remembering that a therapist is never the same to two different clients. Recommendations are just another kind of information to compare with your own ideas of what you want from therapy and from a therapist.

Credentials are not necessarily reliable guidelines, nor is licensing. They tend to be more relevant to the question of social legitimacy, since unconventional therapists often shun traditional educational processes. If you want a therapist who conforms to social standards as a professional and who has a degree, credentials and associations do tell you this. By limiting much of psychotherapy to licensed professionals, under the guise of assuring competency and legitimacy, certain gains are made for professionals. Competition is controlled, ensuring high standards of living, little challenge to the efficacy of professionals, and few changes in the structure and content of professionally dominated institutions. Hence licensing, credentials, and professional associations have more relevance to questions of power and economics. At the moment the field is wide open, and while no one can deny that some nonprofessionals are unhelpful and destructive, the point is that so are many licensed professionals.

Standards for academic credentials and for licensing seem to imply that people know what knowledge, skills, and ethics are necessary to a helpful relationship. But people, including professionals, don't. While there is wide agreement that some therapists are harmful, if you were to ask for specific examples, few therapists would agree on what constitutes "harmful." Exploitation, oppression, and racism are well-known evils, but psychotherapy is far from being able to define these concepts specifically enough to identify therapists who are destructive to their clients.

Until therapists substantially agree on what is harmful or helpful behavior and make these standards explicit, concrete, and widely known, people cannot be sure of getting the best unless they rely on their own intuition, experiences, and judgment. Choosing a therapist who will offer you excellent help cannot be short-cut by credentials, licenses, or professional associations. Therapists who emphasize these aspects of their background, however, will be those who closely identify with the values and aspiriations of the upper middle class, and this makes it relatively easy for clients with similar ideological persuasions and desires to seek them out. For other therapists, credentials may be irrelevant, or "playing the game." They may accept the credential's usefulness economically and socially, despite its irrelevance to standards of excellence and integrity. One can talk about credentials with therapists as a means of feeling out their attitudes toward normative modes of behavior and conventional standards.

The personality of the therapist is far more difficult to assess than any other factor critical in choosing a therapist. First of all, most therapists try to withhold subjective information, trying to achieve an "objective" persona. This is a reflection of psychoanalysis (Freud's method of treatment), which assumed that the primary way a client related to a therapist was through transference. That is, the client acted as if the therapist were someone else, usually a person with whom the client had had an incomplete relationship, such as a parent. Countertransference means "inappropriate" feelings toward a client by a therapist and suggests a "neurotic" (read "unacceptable") tinge. By presenting a bland exterior the therapist fosters the transference. Unfortunately, therapists who deliberately withhold all direct statements about themselves are not "objective," they are seen as cold, withdrawn, and insensitive by many clients. People who act this way in any other relationship would be considered in the same terms. Therefore, the cues from the therapist suggest (in terms of social conventions basic to nonverbal communication) an attitude.

Another difficulty is that therapists tend to place little importance on their relationships to the clients, which include their verbal and nonverbal communications. Surprisingly, therapists act as if their interpretations are the only aspect of their interactions which affect clients and then always either benignly or helpfully. Negative reactions to a therapist are invariably interpreted as entirely the function of the client's psyche, rooted in past experiences or distortions of the present one. That a conclusion so unlikely is so prevalent is strong evidence that therapy is far from being influenced by clinical research, which, despite its many handicaps, continually suggests that therapists whole demeanors affect clients, that body language communicates to clients and influences behavior in ways which are at least as powerful as spoken language, and interpretations have hurtful consequences as well as benign or helpful ones.

Finally, therapists do not view the initial sessions as a time for clients to see their personalities as therapists and make judgments about commitments to therapy. These difficulties are obstacles the client must use (or avoid) in determining which therapist is most suited to what he or she wants to accomplish at that moment.

Clients must decide, if they make decisions about their therapists, four major issues. One, is the therapist's style in itself frustrating and difficult to contend with? Two, is the therapist's method of approaching therapy in line with the way the client would like to participate? Three, is the therapist a person who can be liked, trusted, and respected? Four, does the therapist present him or herself personally to the extent the client needs? The relationship or rapport the client has with the therapist is the single most important factor in *any* successful therapy. Keep this in mind.

Alice goes to a therapist, her fourth, who wears short skirts. Alice likes this because to her it indicates the therapist is "lively." On the other hand, Alice wonders about the complete impersonality of the therapist. She sits, listens, and occasionally makes a reflective comment such as, "You don't like your roommate" after Alice has said, "I don't really get along with my roommate." Alice points out, "If I didn't like her, that's what I would have said." In other words, Alice is much more accurate in her statements than the therapist implies. She would like to know more about the therapist, since she is not yet sure the therapy relationship can progress unless the therapist treats Alice more as a person, rather than the object of a systematic method of therapy. Alice is not content with a "one-down" relationship with a therapist, does not want simply to talk to herself (she is experienced enough with therapy to predict the therapist's reactions), and is anxious for someone to establish personal contact with her. A therapist who will not respond to the individual is impersonal by definition. That such impersonality is not helpful is evident by looking at all the impersonality in the world, all the incidents where the person is treated as an object, and comparing this with the misery. The most prevalent inference is that impersonality leads to psychic stress rather than alleviates it. Yet in the name of scientific objectivity therapists seem to persist in remaining aloof, authoritarian, impersonal, "objective," and dispassionate.

BeJay liked what she heard about a psychiatrist and went to him. She was thrilled to find out he was the kind of man she was eager to have as a psychiatrist—warm, responsive, compassionate. Yet he favored an approach to therapy which involved BeJay in a group. BeJay was terrified by groups because she did not have a firm grip on her own identity—the root of her problem—and therefore she reacted to groups by becoming paranoid and unresponsive. Consequently, his insistence that she join the group created at the beginning of therapy a deep conflict within her between wanting to work on her problems but not wanting to be exposed to them in a way she experienced as overwhelming.

Some therapists might feel that insistence on participation in a group is an appropriate response to someone who fears losing his or her identity in groups, and I agree that this would be part of any therapeutic approach. But by not allowing BeJay to make this choice herself, the therapist precipitated a conflict rather than allowing BeJay to join the group when she was ready. The result was that BeJay left therapy. Some therapists present a demand to a client immediately; the client's refusal to meet the therapist's demands indicates a basic reluctance to engage in a therapy relationship, that is, to attempt to change. BeJay's situation was different: she was thrown into a group because of the therapist's preference for group work, not because the therapist was testing her willingness to work on issues and make changes. His method created her madness.

Often the therapist's direction and comments become increasingly irrelevant to the client's dilemmas, particularly if the therapist's approach is more gratifying for the therapist than helpful to the client. One such example, an unfortunately common one, is the seduction of a woman client into a dependent relationship with a male therapist. The therapist offers warmth, support, uncritical acceptance, indeed, an appealing and intimate relationship. Yet there is always the final limit, particularly for the ethical therapist—no sexual behavior. And there is termination, usually a decision made by the therapist in this situation, not by the client. When the client is dependent on the therapist, she begins having fantasies about sexual relationships with the therapist. Such fantasies are probably common in all therapy relationships, but in the intensely dependent relationship they become obsessions.

The client brings up the fantasies, abasing herself in an attempt to tell the therapist how close she is and wants to become. The therapist accepts the content of the fantasies by acting as if the fantasies are one more symptomatic expression of the client's problems, rather than a direct consequence of the therapist's behavior. The therapist, through the absence of realism in the therapy relationship, has allowed the client to believe he will meet all of her needs. The self-humiliation of the client is terrifying to most therapists, who suddenly do not want to continue the relationship. The demands are too excessive, and the request for a sexual relationship is too dangerous.

By allowing the client to express the sexual desires, as the client was allowed to express any and all other types of feelings, fantasies, and wishes earlier in therapy, the therapist is persuaded that the client's needs for acceptance, affirmation, and regard are being met. Perhaps they are, but with horrendous consequences to the client. The therapists in these situations rarely accept, or are even willing to acknowledge, the intense rage their clients must have toward them. The client has been led to expect that the therapist will meet all her needs, but she suddenly finds the therapist hiding behind roles or ducking out on the relationship. The client is being totally rejected as a person. There is no alternative, for to have sexual relations at this point would only be exploitive. The point is that the therapist can never be, and should never have presented himself to be, a person who can love, support, and uncritically accept the client without reservation. To pretend that this message is helpful, that the induction of dependency is helpful because the therapist can work within the relationship to help the client become independent is self-serving and logically contradictory.

As the relationship nears termination the client's rage and feeling of having been victimized by the therapist is submerged under the therapist's persistent discussion of termination issues, problems outside of therapy, and so forth. Yet the client has no choice at this point: her humiliation at exposing her fantasies for analysis is too complete for her to object to the therapist's maneuvers. The client leaves, in the therapist's eyes a successful case, only to turn her hostility onto others or herself.

Some people need a warm, affectionate therapist who will hold them at times. Others want a therapist who keeps a clear distance between the client and himself or herself, allowing the client to express urges for a relationship which the client realizes are unrealistic, but which need to be expressed. Some therapists can provide either relationship, some, only the latter. Depending on what kind of relationship you want and need, including or excluding talk, touch, sense, or sharing of experiences, feelings, and so forth, you must select a therapist with the capacity for responding to your needs. Perhaps these needs are immature, but without recognizing, expressing, and accepting these needs as an expression of you, they cannot be integrated into yourself, and this integration allows you to become more complete, to grow. For many people, acting in therapy is the only way they can experience and integrate certain areas of their personality. An exclusively verbal relationship is an accent on the area of their strongest defenses—rationalization, intellectualization, debate, mystification. Words are our primary means of defense against unacceptable aspects of ourselves and others, and they are often the least effective, slowest means of changing.

You must decide what characteristics of a therapist as person you need, what ones you want, and what ones you can tolerate even though they are not necessarily desirable. Looking for a therapist who comes closest to meeting these characteristics may postpone therapy work for awhile; but therapy undertaken with someone who is, in fact, alien and unlikable is not helpful, while therapy with a marginally acceptable person tends to be just that, marginal. During the most painful part of therapy the client depends on affection and regard for the therapist to motivate him or her to continue beyond the critical moments. Without a trust in the therapist's judgment, skills, and integrity, the client should not take major risks. If the client attempts to plunge into deep and conflicted waters without a supportive relationship, he or she may drown. Therapy with a therapist who is experienced by the client as insensitive, coercive, seductive, manipulative, obscure, unresponsive, or irrelevant to the client's needs isn't therapy as much as it is a form of self-destruction.

Some therapists will accept a client they do not like, perhaps for economic reasons. Experienced therapists recognize and avoid clients they cannot work with successfully. Few therapists would choose a therapist for themselves without careful consideration of the factors I have been discussing. Therapists who do work with people they don't like or cannot help (because they do not know what help is or because of their own limitations) are rarely helpful, however well-intentioned they may be. Therapists know this and scrutinize anyone they would go see extremely carefully, stressing compatibility of values and outlook, ability to develop rapport, a sense of confidence based on the experience in the first interview, general reputation, background (not credentials), and so forth. Why should clients do less for themselves?

Each individual wants different characteristics in his or her therapist. Sex, for example, has become a major, controversial issue. Some feminists argue that women should only see women therapists. Other feminists say this is often impossible as there are few women therapists, and women should be able to tell which therapists in the area are acceptable for women and which are not. Allowing men to influence the development of a woman's consciousness, if she has had emotionally damaging relationships with men throughout her life, is probably unwise. On the other hand, some women either have had positive relationships with men or would like to and seek a male therapist in order to work these issues out. Others may trust men because they are considered more authoritative, competent, and reliable (more "objective"). Regardless of the reasons for choosing or not choosing male therapists, feminists have touched a very sensitive area. And in choosing a therapist you must consider all relevant factors in the context of your lifestyle and values.

Many women do have deep-seated fears of men. They use many conventional behavior patterns to conceal their feelings, including crying when they are angry, feeling guilty when they are resentful, and so forth. Many problems women have are directly due to sex-role stereotyping and oppression. Working out these issues and being honest with oneself are undoubtedly more difficult to do with a man than with a woman. The consciousness of an individual is a precarious structure, resting on a few basic assumptions from which most of a person's world view, rationales for behavior, and defense system are derived. Many of these basic beliefs are oppressive and therefore harmful to the individual. For example, if a woman is brought up to believe her ultimate role in society is to be a wife and a mother, have children, raise them, take care of the home, and make sacrifices for her husband's well-being, these beliefs are part of her consciousness. When emotions and intuition challenge these beliefs, substantially or in part, inner conflicts result but also radical personality and life style changes become possible. Men may fear changes in these beliefs because their security rests on them. One hears many therapists recommending that women accept their roles as mothers and wives, build families, make sacrifices. Undoubtedly this is neither helpful nor therapeutically appropriate, but the message is delivered in subtle and not so subtle ways.

The underlying issue, a woman's need to accept her emotions, intuition, intellect, and physical being as bases for action in herself, without dependence on men or on social norms, no matter how deeply rooted in her consciousness, is difficult to explore with a male therapist, because he has too much at stake. All his needs may be coming directly (through lovers and wives) or indirectly (from female clients) from women. If a client begins to question her sexually stereotyped assumptions about herself, she will eventually come to question her assumptions about the therapist. And her relationship to the therapist will necessarily become more equalized and less flattering to any need on the therapist's part for a dependent, passive, helpless woman to protect, nourish, validate, and paternalize. At this point the therapist will become defensive, which means aggressively hostile toward the client.

On the other hand, many women therapists have thoroughly absorbed the same basic beliefs men share about women. They, too, will become threatened when challenged and may use their skills as therapists against the client, undermining the client's self-confidence, playing on guilt and shame. Often, indeed, the very same destructive manipulations, short of seduction, are characteristic of some women therapists as well as of men. More depends on the personal qualities of the therapist than on the sex.

Women seeking therapists should not discount feminist objections to male therapists. They range from the extreme cases of physical seduction of clients to the more subtle ways therapists can use interpretation, silence, the client's inner conflicts, emotions, self-contempt, self-doubt, and the powerful need clients have to be highly regarded by their therapists against clients strivings for self-actualization and personal growth and away from oppressive assumptions about women. The emotional and psychic damage done by an oppressive therapist is no less profound and limiting because there is no symbolic act proclaiming the fact of the damage as clearly as seduction does. To know that a client has been seduced by a therapist is to see clearly how a male therapist has attacked a woman, despite some male therapists' arguments that seduction is therapeutic. To find out that a woman has not been able radically to question her fundamental beliefs about what it means to be a woman and what it does not mean in therapy is less obvious. In one case it is what happened, in the other it is what did not happen.

Despite the fact that I am a male therapist and consider myself to be working progressively on what being a man means to me (rather than saying, "I am liberated toward women," which uses women's liberation and its themes as a reference point for a man's personal growth), I believe it is poor judgment for any woman to enter therapy unless—and this qualification is not meant to understate my belief that women should see women therapists—she is simultaneously active in a women's consciousness-raising group and feels free to discuss all aspects of the therapy relationship with close women friends and all aspects of consciousness raising with the therapist. Many women prefer to see male therapists, and most male therapists prefer women clients because men as clients tend to be more competitive and hostile. (It is very difficult for some men to admit they are not in control of a relationship or themselves, and many men are brought into therapy by their wives or lovers; few seek therapy for themselves, only to save a relationship or get women off their backs). But as a therapist it is my responsibility to see that women who come to me as a therapist are not emotionally damaged by the experience, and one way to do this is to insist they develop a support network among other women to explore the therapy relationship on a regular basis and to keep a sense of perspective, if nothing else.

There are other specific considerations to be made in seeking an appropriate therapist. An example is the ideological background of the therapist, specifically, the attitude of the therapist toward the individual's role in society and the relationship of the individual to authority. In short, is the therapist politicized? The radical therapy movement, the left wing of therapy, insists that the individual be considered in terms of the social and political context in which he or she lives. The implication is that people's problems result from oppressive social contexts. If the client doesn't think his or her situation is entirely his or her fault, he or she will want to examine how others relate to him or her and learn how to influence other people's behavior. Learning to satisfy one's needs through others without controlling them is a difficult task.

Going to a therapist who feels that society is essentially sound and that the individual can be allowed some latitude but is better off working through conventional methods and achieving conventional goals doesn't make sense for someone who is challenging marriage as an institution, exploring child raising through contractual agreements with the other parent, living in a commune, using drugs as a means of pleasure and personal growth, exploring deviant subcultures and behavior (being a "street person" or getting into bisexual relations, homosexual relations, or variations on hetereosexual relations). The difficulty is that some therapists present themselves as liberal and tolerant but actually attempt to reduce alternative modes of thinking, feeling, and doing to conventional structures.

Kenny went to a therapist who impressed him as being with it. The therapist accepted Kenny as a homosexual and told Kenny this was an adjustment to sexuality a minority of people made but was neither unnatural nor perverted. Kenny went wild with enthusiasm. He had never met a therapist who accepted his homosexuality. He began to open up, talking about issues which had many emotions attached to them. Suddenly he noticed a striking pattern. The therapist would ask him about intimacy, responsibilities to his lovers, and constancy. He would tell Kenny how "promiscuous" he was and how unsatisfied he must be without a deep relationship with one man. He would suggest that homosexual relationships can never really fulfill a person or offer him the security of a long-term relationship. These standards for the homosexual relationship were not Kenny's; they were the conventional standards for heterosexual relationships with the object of matrimony. Kenny didn't want a long-term relationship with one man. He enjoyed homosexuality because it introduced a new dimension to his relationships with men, allowing him more completely satisfying relationships. He did not want to be anyone's possession, nor did he want to possess anyone. Intimacy was, indeed, part of all of his relationships, without the overtones of possessiveness or exclusiveness. The therapist could accept homosexuality only as far as the homosexual relationship manifested all the structure and values of heterosexual relationships: when only the sex of the love object differed but in all other respects the relationship conformed to conventional standards and appearances.

Jimmy, Eric, Sara, and Linda lived together with four other people in a commune. Difficulties in their relationships with the other people in the house prompted them to talk everyone into inviting a therapist into the commune to help them out. They knew a professor of psychology who was interested in their commune and was eager to consult. He began by coming to weekly meetings where people could talk about emotionally sensitive issues openly. This led some people to express hostility toward two members of the commune. The hostility was interpreted as scapegoating, as there were no signs in the group that the couple (Eric and Sara) deserved the hostilities. Unfortunately, Eric and Sara were difficult to live with outside the group. They were constantly hostile and contemptuous toward everyone else. Their relationship with each other was volatile and erratic, but they never allowed it to be a topic of general conversation, despite its consistantly deleterious effects on everyone else. Neither could be depended upon, ever; both made continual demands on everyone.

When group members mentioned these points, Eric and Sara explained that the same behavior patterns were characteristic of others in the commune. They agreed these were accurate descriptions of some of the things they did, but they couldn't understand why they were singled out for blame. The therapist, reducing the dynamics of a living situation involving many levels of interactions throughout the day to the dynamics evident to him during a meeting, sided with

Eric and Sara, interpreting attacks on them as irresponsible. Had the therapist lived in the commune for a period of time, rather than assuming that understanding of the dynamics of the group could come from weekly meetings, the critical fact that Eric and Sara were constantly demanding, never satisfying of others' needs, always using other people or ignoring them completely would have been clear. Eric and Sara pretended in the group meeting to be sharing, contributing members of the commune. In any group meeting, since there is no evidence of what people really do, any and every claim appears equally valid. The therapist did not have the sympathy or empathy toward communal living which told him the other group members were expressing a real issue between themselves and Eric and Sara. He did not have the experience of living in a commune, nor did he consider this necessary to being able to grasp the essential issues. Unfortunately, theories of group dynamics are not based on real life group situations, but on abstract, artificial gatherings (meetings) with finite limits; therefore, they are not always reflective of every group issue. Again, the therapist reduced the alternative lifestyle to a conventional frame of reference without realizing, despite the best of intentions, that this reduction was oppressive to the commune.

Life experiences are influential in the therapist's approach to a client's difficulties. While it is not true that a therapist must have experienced the client's problem himself or herself to be helpful, I believe the therapist must have dealt with some kinds of problems in his or her own life to be fully empathetic to the anguish the client feels and to the subtleties of the situation. Loss of loved ones through death, divorce, and forced separations are common experiences, and the pain involved, as well as the fear created by anticipated loss, can easily be minimized by a person who has not had analogous experiences in his or her own life. The more the experiences, relationships, change processes in the therapist's own life include the kinds of difficulties posed by clients, the greater the degree of empathy. A therapist, for example, who is happily married with friends and relatives who are happily married, confronting a couple on the verge of divorce, may not be able to recognize and affirm the validity of divorce as a solution to the couple's conflicts. That is not to say that a therapist must be divorced, only familiar with divorce in a human and personal, rather than academic way. The therapist should be familiar with the problems of living in our society as a person, not just through literature. The difference, I suppose, is between knowledge about and knowledge of a situation. To the client, a therapist who lives a varied and rich life and who draws on personal experience for metaphors and as a basis for empathy is preferable to a therapist who has only read about other people's problems.

Rick is a therapist interested in alternative lifestyles, particularly communes. He personally never wanted to live in a commune; but he was fascinated by the problems and solutions occuring in communes he was familiar with, so he joined a cooperative living house for a six-month period. This experience allowed him to realize how complex communal living is and how little his intellectual background prepared him for dealing with communes. He then read many books on the subject, talked intensively with people who lived in communes, and spent time visiting communes until he was an accepted face. Finally, after two or three years of preparing to deal with communal living situations, he offered to consult with a recently formed commune.

His approach was to talk first with individuals about the hassles they were experiencing, then to talk with small, natural groups. When he discovered an issue coming up throughout these conversations, he would talk with people experienced in communal living but outside the house about the issue. Then he would present his viewpoint on the particular issue, drawing on conversations in and out of the house as well as on group dynamics to illustrate the way this issue manifested itself in the commune. After identifying the issue, he outlined several alternative ways of approaching and resolving it. This led to stimulating, specific discussions in the group, without anyone blaming anyone else for the problem but recognizing that all contributed to the difficulties. He used this approach with Eric and Sara, persuading them that the group had a valid and unique statement to make about them, despite their belief that everyone else acted the same way. Rick brought up examples where everyone else acted differently, identified the differences, and pointed out how rarely Eric and Sara acted differently from the way people perceived them: hostile, exploitive, contemptuous of others. In this context Eric and Sara could hear the group finding occasions ("rare") where they acted more supportively, openly, and cooperatively. Eric and Sara stopped fighting the group's attempt to influence their behavior, while not feeling compelled to act differently. The group, having had their rage validated, could begin to differentiate without feeling that their central concern was being dismantled. They could be more supportive, less judgmental, and consequently could look at the ways their reactions to Eric and Sara added to the pattern everyone found unsatisfying.

The importance here is that Rick identified with the communal experience, recognizing that intellectually alone he could not hope to grasp the emotional dilemmas people were struggling with. He had to draw on his own experiences in communal living, other people's experiences, and time in the commune relating to everyone without the artificial structure of the meetings before he could offer a perspective solid enough people could work with it. It is not enough for therapists to be tolerant they must be involved in experiences of changes, experimentation, risk taking, loneliness, and loss in order to have personalities genuinely broad enough to empathize with clients as peers, rather than constrict them into the role of "patients."

Sex, experiences, maturity, and ideology affect any therapy relationship, from the classic psychoanalyst sitting behind a couch to the encounter group leader fighting with a member in the middle of the group. They are critical influences on a relationship where disparities, incongruities, and contradictions inevitably show the client to the therapist and the therapist to the client. Invariably people who have selected a therapist without weighing these factors to the best possible extent find themselves caught in a relationship with clear, oppressive limits they don't know how to deal with in the sessions. It is not too extreme to say that the client's resistance in therapy is not entirely related to intrapsychic phenomenon, but to factors about the therapist and the relationship the therapist is not looking for and the client doesn't want to or isn't able to articulate.

The cliché, therapists have to be a little crazy to work with crazy people, has, as all clichés do, some truth to it. Without experiences of pain (terror, hate, helplessness, utter confusion, loneliness) the therapist may describe the client in brilliant, elegant terms but cannot come to grips with the client's agony. And without sharing with the client the responses which come from knowing pain, the therapist cannot develop a deep rapport and trust with the client.

5
The Therapy Relationship

People going into therapy want to know what psychotherapy is like, but there are no definitive answers to this question. Much depends on the people involved and what each brings to the relationship. However it should be possible to isolate some factors which may provide the basic guidelines necessary for making as many of the decisions involved with the therapy process as explicitly and deliberately as possible.

Ordinarily clients use the first session to discuss the problems they feel are causing their difficulties. Partly because they want relief as quickly as possible, partly because they think the therapist expects them to explain why they have come to psychotherapy as fully as possible, most clients submerge the questions they have about psychotherapy. This is a mistake. The best way to use the first session is to outline, with the therapist, the basis for the psychotherapy relationship.

Developing a therapy contract may take a few minutes or more than one session. Yet without an explicit and thoroughly acceptable contract, the client is at a severe disadvantage. Participating in psychotherapy on trust in the benevolent expertise of the therapist is quite possibly to open oneself up to a process which may be not just unhelpful, but damaging.

Begin by asking the therapist questions about him or herself. Questions about the therapist's personal beliefs, values, background, and personality are appropriate. Many therapists will resist answering questions relating to their beliefs or competence and try to throw this back onto the client by saying, "Didn't you come here to discuss your problems?" Don't be misled. You are there first to decide if this person is someone you can work well with, not to expose yourself to a stranger on the basis of blind trust in his or her professional status. You are paying this person. This does not give you the right, of course to explore the therapist's personal life. It does give you the right to find out the therapist's values, background relevant to psychotherapy, point of view regarding peoples' problems, approach to therapy (methods), and so forth.

In asking about the methods of the therapist expect some vague statements like, "I'm eclectic," or "I use whatever seems appropriate." Persist; try to find out more precisely what the therapist feels are valid or invalid approaches to conflict situations or emotional problems a client has.

Generally, the three major approaches are verbal, experiential, and nonverbal. Verbal approaches include analysis, discussion, the use of interpretation, challenges, and arguments. Sometimes the therapist may be didactic, giving the client information regarding an area of difficulty. Experiential approaches focus on the client's acting out some portion or all of a particular situation. Gestalt therapy, role playing, and psychodrama are examples of experiential approaches to psychotherapy, but keeping journals, doing "homework," and drawing are others. Nonverbal approaches may involve meditation, but more usually they involve physical exercises and massage. Some therapists use the confusion surrounding nonverbal methods to disguise sexual exploitation of their clients. It is important to have the therapist clarify his or her preferences beforehand and explain why he or she uses one method rather than another. If the therapist in the initial interview never mentions making physical contact (aside from appropriate, therefore nonanxiety-provoking gestures of support or affection which would never be concealed from an outsider) but suggests this when you are well into the therapy relationship, you may simply say, "No, this isn't part of the contract." Any attempt by the therapist to alter the contract then would be justification to stop therapy.

Many therapists remain strictly focused on verbal exchanges. If you are skillful at manipulating people verbally or intellectualizing about emotionally significant events in your life, experiential therapy may be more helpful, since you act out situations. Involving physical movements (body language), emotions, words, fantasies, and images (sometimes "alter egos") in the therapy process makes it less likely you will be able to avoid expressing and becoming aware of contradictions between what happens and how you want to perceive what is happening. This means that experiential learning may be not only more dramatic and exciting, but more painful and difficult to integrate. Sensibilities may be upset or damaged in exclusively experiential experiences, and clients who are largely verbal might want to try a primarily verbal method until they are secure with themselves and have developed ways to integrate emotional material, graduating to experiential methods at that point.

Each method may focus on different elements in the individual, such as feelings, images, dreams, muscles, sexual activities, relationships with others, personal history, immediate crises and precipitating incidents, and so forth. Topics of discussion will range far more widely than will the therapist's comfort and expertise in dealing therapeutically with the issues. The client may select a method which is most similar to his or her usual approach to problem solving and work toward other methods with other therapists at later times. A good rule to keep in mind is that the therapists specializing in physical contact methods (exercises, massage, and so forth) are specialists, with extensive training in physiology (although not necessarily in medicine). Their ideological or theoretical background will include Wilhelm Reich, Otto Rank, and others. Almost without exception therapists using these methods decry verbal approaches or at least, have nothing to do with them themselves. And they necessarily maintain appropriate limits within the scope of physical contact.

There are no methods or theories which suggest that sexual relations between client and therapist are therapeutic. They may be pleasant, rewarding, meaningful, significant expressions of mutual regard, or they may be crass exploitations of therapist by client or client by therapist. A client may decide to have a sexual relationship with a therapist without being psychologically damaged by the relationship, assuming the client does not mystify the sexuality as "therapy" or accept the suggestion by the therapist that it is part of the therapy relationship. Sexual relationships between client and therapist must be regarded as a separate kind of relationship, to be judged by the individuals involved according to the same terms by which any sexual relationship is judged. Also, clients should realize the involvement of a client with a therapist as a friend or lover may be grounded in the events of the therapy relationship but may move beyond them. Therapy per se ends when friendship (equal symmetrical relationships) or love begins.

Therapy has never begun when a client or therapist succeeds in manipulating the other into acting out (but without a theoretical system available to detect and eliminate self-deception) compulsive mastery-submission games and other oppressive rituals of interactions.

Once the client is clear about the questions and answers he or she has about the therapist and the method, he or she will begin to feel more comfortable talking with the therapist. The therapist will also feel comfortable discussing the therapy relationship with the client. Otherwise the therapist will talk at the client, who will listen passively, and make conventional responses. Imagine discussing the length of therapy, scheduling of sessions, fees, termination, in other words, the structure of therapy, with a therapist with whom you could not feel comfortable in making your point of view known or asserting your limits. The therapist would take charge with your tacit approval, and you would end up oppressed by the therapy relationship.

If you are oppressed by the terms of the therapy, this will lead to submerged resentments. Perhaps these resentments will surface as missed appointments (for which many patients are charged) or through the withholding of important information from the therapist. At any rate resentment toward therapy and the therapist is self-defeating. To the extent it is caused by the negotiation of the contract, it can be avoided if you know your rights and needs and stand up for them.

The negotiation of the contract should take precedence over the in-depth discussion of the problems bringing the client into therapy. Many therapists are trained to find out what led the client to seek therapy at that particular time, which begs the contract question. The assumption seems to be that if a client comes to therapy, he or she wants therapy with the therapist he or she is being interviewed by. Facile assumptions are rarely helpful or accurate. Many clients are, in fact, ambivalent about therapy and want to see what the relationship would entail. Others, more sure of therapy, are not convinced the particular therapist or method is what they want. The first interview is primarily a searching out of their questions and doubts, and when therapist and client try to do this while talking about the problems that brought the client into therapy, confusion results. Clients often put off their questions and may choose to avoid future sessions, manipulate around unacceptable limits, or express submerged resentments indirectly.

The length of therapy can never be anticipated as there are too many variables which affect the outcome. However, if therapy is, at least in theory, interminable, the client is faced with many difficulties. First, there may never come a time when the therapist (who is earning a comfortable, secure living from clients) suggests that the client is ready to leave therapy. Second, the client may eventually fade out of therapy never fully dealing with completion, just losing stamina. Third, the client may become dependent on the regularity of sessions and never resist interminable therapy. Fourth, the client has no basis to decide when, and if, therapy has proven to be ineffectual with this particular therapist.

A better approach might be to agree to an arbitrary end point. My rules of thumb are five to six sessions for crisis intervention, six months to a year for major difficulties involving many aspects of the clients life, and a year or two for complete analysis of the individual. A client involved in a family crisis or a problematic relationship with someone else may find therapy most often lasts three to four months. These figures are based on an average of one and a half hours a week. A client can therefore make a commitment based on his or her goals: to ten sessions (maximum), to three or four months (maximum), to six months, to a year, to more. These arbitrary end points give the client several advantages and no disadvantages (since at the end of the period the client can renegotiate with the therapist for a new contract if desired.

By knowing the commitment is for a specific length of time, barring unforseen difficulties in one's circumstances or clearly unacceptable behavior on the therapist's part, the client is in a better position to recognize that an acute desire to end therapy before the time is up may be resistance to completing the agreement, hence to working on some unconscious, repressed issues. Without an end point, the desire to terminate may be a reflection of futility, rejection of the efficacy of therapy, a sense the work is completed, and so forth. On the other hand, a client may prefer to keep the length of therapy open and focus on goals, so that once the goals are achieved, he or she will be able to leave therapy. The difficulty with this position is in the ambiguity of most goals: clients may deceive themselves into thinking they have reached their goals, when all they are doing is rationalizing escape from anxiety-provoking explorations into areas of repressed awareness and emotional conflicts.

Another advantage of a definite end point is that it gives clients a sense of therapy as a finite relationship, regardless of the complexity and unresolved qualities of many of their personal themes and issues. Therapy is best seen as one way people can explore aspects of their lives, not as the exclusive solution to their dilemmas. Many times successful therapy leaves the individual with problems, but also with a greater capacity to continue working on the resolution of these difficulties. Clients do not become overwhelmed with the complexities of their personalities when they know how long they are committed to exploration and can begin working, at some point, on closure. That is, they can attempt after awhile to reintegrate the different strands of thoughts, emotions, or behavior explored in therapy and get ready to terminate on the prescribed day. A client who knows the time limits may be inclined to focus more on areas of importance rather than circumventing issues or making smalltalk.

Finally, after a period of time has elapsed, the client can legitimately question the effectiveness or value of therapy without feeling guilty. Many clients sense that the therapy process is neither desirable nor valuable but cannot bring themselves to terminate, fearing the therapist's adverse reaction. By having a fixed limit, clients can gracefully withdraw, knowing they have fulfilled their commitment to a specific length of time, even if their interest has waned. It is important to use the arbitrary time limit to one's advantage, not to allow it to dominate oneself. One can always renegotiate therapy if the relationship has proved helpful and effective and if there are specific goals which can be accomplished by doing so.

If you have doubts about the therapist, agree to a short enough period of therapy to give him or her a chance to demonstrate his or her abilities (and cooperate with therapy unreservingly or you undermine the process, despite the skills and intentions of the therapist) and then renegotiate for longer periods if you so desire. Many clients prefer to deal with a crisis, see how the therapist is able to help them during this crisis, and then negotiate for longer, more intensive work. Some therapists are particularly helpful during crises, while being less inclined to work with long-term therapy relationships.

Next, focus contract negotiations on the question of schedule. Find times which are agreeable to both you and the therapist. Many therapists (and clients) function better early in the day, others later on, some best in the evenings. A therapy session early in the week may be a drag, while later in the week it may seem a welcome relief from pressures, depending on mood swings and lifestyles. Find two or three optimal times for scheduling a session and offer the therapist these possibilities, rather than fitting into his or her schedule. The more you take the initiative and are able to meet your own needs through therapy—structure and content—the more helpful the process will be. The more you allow yourself to be passive and compliant, the more likely it is you will find therapy itself an obstacle to enjoyment. For example, if you look forward to Friday afternoons as a time to relax, don't schedule a therapy session then. It will take away from time you need to enjoy yourself. On the other hand, if Friday is a time you take to begin addressing your personal needs (rather than "working") therapy may be a way of starting off the weekend well.

Few therapists have questioned the appropriateness of hour-long sessions. This time limit has no relationship to what is best for the therapy process. I have found people warm up in the first three-quarters of an hour, get into an issue toward the end of the first hour, and often bring it to a successful and natural resolution in an hour and a half. Consequently, this is the average session, while some last only an hour, others two, even three hours or more (during crises). Some therapists feel an hour is adequate time since it forces clients to organize their time and present their material and does not give them a chance to manipulate for extra time as a way of gaining indirect signs of therapists' approval, affection, or gullibility. I don't like to force clients at all, and no client has ever given me the impression he or she has deliberately stretched a session beyond the usual ending time in order to express feelings toward me or therapy. Many clients complain bitterly, outside of therapy, of being arbitrarily cut off at the end of an hour with total disregard to what they were feeling or trying to deal with and going home only to force friends, lovers, relatives, or spouses to cope with the often negative effects of the unfinished business.

Fees are a controversial issue. Many therapists find therapy sessions, overall, an emotional drain. They expect and, realistically, need compensation for the time, energy, and skills they use during therapy, in addition to any intrinsic reward for being helpful. Besides earning a living, there are many benefits which come from assuming the therapist's role. One gains prestige, a sense of self-worth, power, security, and social identity from the role. Clients, on the other hand, usually suffer a loss of self-esteem, a sense of being inadequate for having to seek help, insecurity, dependency on the therapist, and a loss of income (to the degree they pay for therapy).

What is an acceptable fee? Again, there is no definitive answer. While it is true that therapists often earn incomes considerably higher than those of their clients, unless they are employed by an agency or institution, this does not necessarily mean they are exploiting their clients. However, if a client is unsatisfied with the results of therapy, whatever he or she has paid will feel exorbitant. A good rule of thumb to follow in negotiating fees (some therapists, however, do not negotiate fees) is to settle on an amount which you can both afford and can see as an investment. Therapy is an investment in your own growth and capability to enjoy living. As with any investment there will be both immediate and long-range gains. If therapy is successful in an immediate sense, the investment is probably going to turn out all right. If not, therapy may be a poor investment (at least at that time, with that therapist).

There is no relationship between the cost of therapy and its quality. Many high-priced therapists trade on credentials, locations, and the mystique of psychotherapy with relatively moderate effectiveness. Social workers average twenty dollars a session; psychiatrists and psychologists charge between thirty-five and fifty dollars a session, not because social workers are inferior therapists, but because their prestige is lower. Generally, fees are based on what the market will bear. The "sliding scale" (what the client can afford based on income and dependents) insures that the therapist gets as much as he or she can.

Considering the ambiguous nature of therapy and the risks involved, not to mention the poorly defined goals (hence lack of evaluative critertia) high fees are probably unjustified. Look for the best therapist on your terms, and if you find one you like, then be prepared to make a considerable financial investment in your well-being with reasonable certainty the investment is a good risk. The poorer you are the more expensive, relatively speaking, will be your therapy both in proportion to your income and in terms of the bureaucratic procedures and humiliations often involved in contacts with agencies and institutions (where good therapists can often be found). Therapy is not inexpensive. There is a growing concern among radical therapists like myself that people do not end up "fined" for having problems in living. People like myself have adjusted our standards of living to below what our peers often earn, in order to provide high-quality (we hope) service for amounts people can afford without pain.

When many professionals have discovered that I prefer to charge fees which are often less than half what they charge, for longer sessions, their reactions tend to fall into three categories. First, some wonder if the low fees give clients the impression that what they are getting is of lesser value. Second, some suggest, by innuendo, that I should be charging less because I'm a nonprofessional. Third, some say I am not taking care of myself well enough, in other words, that I am letting people take advantage of me. I think these responses are all fallacious and based upon a regrettably crude understanding of people.

When I offer clients a therapy relationship which they experience as an intense, positive, learning experience, then they feel the therapy is of value. When I don't, then they don't. The attitude that therapy is worthwhile or not is based on what the experience is like. If I were to charge high fees and provide meaningless therapy, then the clients would be forced to justify their time and the results by pointing out how much the therapy costs, implying that the high fees were proof, despite their personal experience, that the therapy was valuable. In strict economic terms anything which costs a great deal is valuable. To justify therapy by charging high fees seems to be exploitive and alienated from the authentic values people can derive from experience.

My nonprofessional status, if it is that, doesn't keep me from charging higher fees any more than it keeps clients from paying. Indeed, they expect to pay much more than I charge for therapy. My fees are low by choice. My lifestyle is also set by choice. I have deliberately worked out a lifestyle which offers to me the maximum amount of pleasure, meaning, and purpose. And at the same time, it is a lifestyle which does not depend on maintaining a standard of living which in itself becomes a burden. I know several therapists who earn more than $50,000 a year, but because of alimony, the upkeep of their possessions, fluctuations in caseloads, the need to charge high consulting fees, indeed, the compulsive need to maintain the lifestyle because of built-in obligations, they end up miserable and strained. They are often unable to enjoy themselves, to explore new areas of experience, to be mobile and flexible. Just as high fees don't guarantee the quality of therapy, high incomes don't, in themselves, guarantee a satisfying existence.

Eventually, as therapy becomes demystified, many people who are neither professionals nor competent will claim to be psychotherapists. Some of these people will be after money, some prestige, others power. Of course, many people become professionals for the same reasons. The risks increase for the prospective clients in direct proportion to the needs of men and women to interpret and clarify experience, to explore the mysteries of existence. Building professional elites who are accorded high standards of living, prestige, and personal power seems to be antithetical to the humane goals of psychotherapy.

A final element in the contract is the issues and goals of psychotherapy. The more specific the agreement is, the more likely these goals can be reached and the issues explored. However, this is the part of the contract which may take a great deal of time, as the initial presentation of the client is usually not the mutually agreed upon conclusions of therapist and client. But once the structure of therapy—length of the relationship, scheduling, methods (ground rules), fees, duration of each session—is resolved, the work of therapy may begin with the exploration of the issues and themes basic to the individual's or family's (married couple's) problems and at the same time goals may be negotiated. Once the client has agreed upon the therapy relationship and has negotiated with the therapist on the structure of the relationship, an exchange, taking off from whatever the client presents and modified by the contributions of the therapist, should fairly soon clarify the issues and goals enough so the contract can be finished. The idea is for the client and therapist to agree on what constitutes the primary focus of the therapy relationship.

In crisis intervention the crisis itself is usually sufficiently extreme to make the underlying issues relatively clear or, at least, close to the surface. The client, anxious to resolve the crisis and given the support and clarification offered by the therapist, is usually particularly open to the issues; so the goals of the relationship are relatively quickly defined. Usually the client must make decisions about what to do, and these decisions or the alternative choices are outlined by the therapist, discussed with the client, and eventually narrowed down to the most suitable options.

In therapy focusing on wider issues and themes, for example, relationships with other people, clients often come in during or following a crisis but with the intention of exploring the area fully, rather than just making decisions necessary to pull themselves out of the particular situation. The difference in terms of content may not be evident at first, but the overall conduct of therapist and client will vary according to their agreement to work on a particular crisis or on themes and related issues. Consequently, it is important for this decision to be made and, if changed, to be changed explicitly and deliberately, not by a gradual merging of crisis intervention with long-term therapy.

The distinction is real because the clients who are seduced into extending the exploration from a crisis into the underlying themes and then realize they are much further into the area than they desire, will find themselves in a difficult and usually self-damaging dilemma. On the one hand, the clients will feel a desire to pursue the issues to the point of resolution; on the other hand, they will feel in over their heads. When caught up in this process, clients often mention feeling worse because they went into therapy. They can pretend to want to continue, while undermining and resisting the efforts of the therapist to do so. Or they can simply drop out of therapy with the issues unresolved and be caught up in an unfinished business syndrome (confused, resentful, anxious, hostile, withdrawn, contradictory). Rarely can they clarify their own dilemmas enough to tell a therapist, "We have gone beyond my limits with this problem: I want my crisis resolved and the underlying issues left alone."

The tendency of many therapists is to resist giving the kind of help a client requests when the therapist is aware of unconscious material the client cannot or will not acknowledge. This creates an estrangement often leading to despair in the client. If a client finds himself or herself in a therapy relationship where the therapist seems reluctant to give the kind of help the client is asking for (advice, clear definitions of the choices and potential consequences facing the client, support, personal opinion), it is often due to the therapist's awareness of underlying issues. Nevertheless, the estrangement is counterproductive. To a client crisis situations are drastic, and he or she wants immediate support, structure, and guidance. To a therapist, believing that the underlying issues will only lead to further crises unless they are worked through, the terms the client establishes for being helped seem self-defeating. This is one of many kinds of conflicts which occur frequently between clients and therapists. The gulf between the therapist's intellectual awareness of the client's difficulties and the client's experientially based needs and desires is one of the most significant. One resolution of such differences may be for the therapist to offer the kind of immediate interventions the client is ready for, mentioning his or her belief that the underlying issues the client is unwilling to deal with may be critical to the problem. Then the client is able to test the therapist's assumptions by seeing if indeed, therapy on those terms was helpful or not. Some therapists will simply refuse to continue therapy unless the client deals with the resistance the therapist perceives to be an obstacle to treatment, but this seems an unduly harsh and uncooperative position. Clients open to changing their understanding of what help is will fare better in these situations during crisis intervention. But the therapist must keep in mind the difference between accepting a crisis for therapy and accepting a long-term client: some things are best left alone until the proper circumstances present themselves.

Determining the goals as soon as possible and making them limited goals if ambiguity or uncertainty exists allows the client, once the goals are reached, to either stop or renegotiate. Yet at the same time, work has to be accomplished even to determine these goals.

The formulation of the contract, gives the client a definite concept of what the structure and goals of the therapy relationship are. At this point the client's major obligation is to work on the issues and themes developed in the exchanges between therapist and client, recognizing that the therapist functions primarily as a guide, not as an arbitrator of the client's consciousness. To expect answers or moral judgments from the therapist, to desire the therapist to meet the emotional, psychic, or physical needs of the client, to expect or demand that the therapist fix blame for the client's misery, to attempt to gain mastery over the therapist, or simply to sit back and let the therapist do all the work are common responses to therapy. But therapy will not be helpful unless clients, within the terms of their contracts, take risks, extend themselves, reflect on the process, and assume as much responsibility for themselves as possible.

6
Is Therapy Helpful?

No question in the field of psychology is more controversial than this one. Clinical research has spiritedly challenged therapists' claims to be helpful. Although this research has been challenged, at the moment prospective clients should realize that many people who have gone through therapy have found it to be either minimally helpful or not helpful at all. Some people, find therapy has been destructive. I believe therapy is helpful under certain conditions, although providing evidence is close to impossible.

I have already mentioned the importance of the client seriously thinking about the expectations he or she has for psychotherapy and, while being open to altering these expectations, moving deliberately toward realizing his or her objectives in therapy. Most importantly, clients must select therapists with whom they have rapport and, depending on what kind of therapy they want, ideological similarities. Furthermore, clients must take an active part in therapy, making their needs known and working with therapists to define a mutually acceptable relationship. The more deliberate and conscious this effort is, the less one has to rely on the skills and sensitivity of the therapist. It is possible, if the client is indirectly and unconsciously cuing the therapist, that the therapists may pick up the cues and respond in helpful ways. But the more people are dependent on therapists to help them define the relationship or the more dependent they are on outside forces to choose their therapists, the more likely it is that the therapy will be minimally helpful. Bluntly, the most disturbed or crazy people run the biggest risks in therapy. Their helplessness makes them vulnerable, and their vulnerability makes them more defensive and resistant to any relationship. This means that the skills of the therapist are crucial, and many therapists are not that skilled, although usually they are well-intentioned.

The way to approach the question of how therapy is helpful is to describe the therapy process. I have isolated four paradoxes which occur and the successive resolutions of these apparent contradictions make the therapy effective, in every therapy situation. I have not outlined the methods every kind of therapy uses to deal with the paradoxes but instead have suggested how some representative therapy approaches do.

THE FIRST PARADOX[1]

A family of four enters therapy. The mother is the first to speak. She explains the problem: her son Norman's inability to make decisions for himself. This is called "the presenting problem," the way a client perceives his or her difficulties. The therapist observes that both children are in their twenties. The mother has brought the entire family into therapy presuma-

[1] The concept of paradox in the psychotherapy relationship has been developed in strikingly disimilar ways by Shelly Kopp [Shelly Kopp, *If You Meet the Buddha on the Road, Kill Him* (Ben Lomond, California: Science & Behavior Books, Inc., 1972).] and Jay Haley [Jay Haley, *Strategies of Psychotherapy* (New York: Grune & Stratton, Inc., 1963).]. Paradox is essential to the work of Don Jackson, Gregory Bateson, and others in the development of the double-bind theory of schizophrenia. Each has had an influence on my thinking, which I both appreciate and wish to acknowledge.

bly because Norman can't make decisions. It is evident the mother makes most, if not all, the decisions in the family. Consequently, the therapist perceives the problem to be more than Norman's "inability" to make decisions. In fact, what will usually emerge in therapy is the fact that Norman can make decisions but doesn't for a variety of reasons, primarily that his mother makes decisions for him and punishes him for initiative.

The differences between the client's perspective of the problem and the therapist's does not mean that the perspectives are mutually exclusive. Certainly the clients believe they are right and resist direct attempts on therapists' parts to redefine the situation. Therapists must accept clients' points of view while simultaneously leading them to change their original perspectives. The resolution of this apparent contradiction is a primary task of therapy.

Depending on how narrow the therapist's point of view is, he or she will perceive the problem of Norman and his family differently. By accepting the mother's formulation the therapist might perceive Norman as having an inability to make decisions and probably other deficiencies in his personality as well. He does depend excessively on his mother, for example, and is immature by social standards. Norman would require considerable work moving him toward maturity and independence by helping him gain insight into his personality and helping him express his feelings more directly.

On the other hand, the therapist may not accept the mother's perspective immediately. He or she may regard the interaction between the two as the problem. If the mother is alternately controlling her son and punishing his initiative, it is unlikely he will resist, particularly if her controls over his life satisfy many of his needs. Indeed, the mother feeds him, clothes him, and gives him shelter and enough room so he rarely feels constricted. He has the illusion of autonomy through a part-time job (his money is superfluous so he can indulge himself) and his car. The major conflict between the mother and son is over his choice of a woman friend. At the age of twenty-nine Norman met a woman he liked and had his first serious relationship. The mother responded by disparaging the woman and chastising her son. She found her own home "invaded" by "the likes of this girl" whom she "couldn't stand being around."

Other therapists would step even further back and suggest that the family as a social system has problems. The sister, Terri, is twenty-six and still living at home. The father is never home except to eat and sleep and has had no involvement with the raising of the children. The mother states very clearly, "The only real fight he and I ever had was over the way I was raising Norman, but I had my way." The mother admits not being able to relate to the father: "I never am allowed to express my anger at him to him. I have to keep it inside." From this point of view all the relationships among the members of the family have disrupted the normal family cycle and caused this family to become stuck. Ordinarily children grow up, mature to some extent in the process, and leave home, attempting and for the most part succeeding in separating from the parents. In this case the children have chronologically become adults, but they remain immature, self-centered, and dependent. More important, they are still at home.

One cannot say that any of these perspectives is right or wrong. But is it not likely that the larger the perspective the greater chance therapy will be effective? Consider the narrowest perspective, that the problem is an inadequate Norman, that something is wrong within him. The symptoms, or signs of difficulty, may be construed to point to this conclusion. After all, he is still at home, dependent on his parents, and unable to take the initiative for his own life. Is it likely a therapist will be able to succeed in helping Norman change when the mother is constantly attempting to control him, seducing him into dependency by gratifying his needs? Besides, Norman didn't come in because he was upset with his situation; his mother brought him in for help. He lacks motivation.

By assuming that the entire family is stuck in one phase of a cycle, the therapist can use the fact that the son and daughter are still at home as a sign that everyone is involved in the problem. The fact that the mother has sought help for her son but has volunteered the entire family and has specifically described her discontent with her husband and her concern that "something is wrong" with both children (a statement she makes in a quiet, offhand way) offers the therapist further material to use in dealing with the entire family. The father and mother can be encouraged to work on their relationship; Terri and Norman can be encouraged to think about moving out on their own. The therapist can begin making the mother's control less satisfying and more frustrating by suggesting she "give in less" to Norman's demands he be taken care of, in order to assist him in growing up. This approach takes into account the mother's self-esteem (she wants to be a good mother, although she defines "good" as completely taking care of her children). The therapist can also support Norman's leaving home and making his own life by suggesting he would be happier on his own. He can relate to any woman he wants in any way he wants without having his mother interfere. This approach deals with all members of the family without blaming any of them, particularly the victim, Norman. There is nothing wrong with Norman from this point of view. The trouble each member has is a function of the way each relates to the other members of the family. The relationship pattern is basically normal but has been carried to an extreme. There need be nothing "wrong" with any individual. They all have made the mistake of relying on one series of relationships, the family, as their primary means of satisfying all their needs and have reduced their flexibility, support network, and opportunities in the process.

Regardless of the perspective of the therapist, the original definition of the problem by the mother will undergo expansion. Some clients present a general problem: "I don't know what is wrong with me. Nothing seems right." This is too vague and all-inclusive to give either the therapist or the client a means of resolving the difficulty. Instead of enlarging the perspective the therapist must specify the problems, while still accepting on the surface the client's perspective that everything is wrong. Eventually therapy may reveal that some things are very wrong, and because they are so wrong, all else appears wrong. As these specific problems are dealt with, the client's appreciation of other aspects of his or her life may improve. No matter what the perspective of the therapist is, the original "problem" must be modified, and this is one of the central tasks of therapy.

The resolution of the contradiction between the therapist's perspective on the problem and the client's is not the client's eventual agreement with the therapist, "Yes, this is my problem, not what I originally thought." When the family described here reaches the point where they all agree they have a problem as a family (assuming the therapist has this perspective), the therapist has by then redefined the problem as well. He or she now is focused on the difficulties in dealing with the complexity of the interrelationships without hurting anyone more than necessary. (Change involves certain amounts of anguish). In other words, when the clients discover the contradiction exists and seek to end the contradiction by accepting the therapist's point of view, they begin to discover the therapist has changed his or her point of view. The contradiction exists throughout therapy until the therapist and client agree that whatever the problems are, the client will be able to cope with them without therapy. Until that point, the therapist's concept of "the problem" and the client's concept of "the problem" will continually change.

THE SECOND PARADOX

Finding out what the problems are is just one theme in any therapy relationship. The second paradox occurs when the therapist attempts to create the prerequisites for change or actual changes. That therapy is change is a truism with much truth. One kind of change will be a redefinition of the "problem"; other kinds of changes may occur in attitudes, relationships, perspectives, understanding, lifestyles, and social contexts (family, school, work, home). The apparent contradiction occurs because clients do not want to change, although they come to therapy because they do not like the way things are. If clients simply wanted to change, therapists might give them advice which they could experiment with to see if it worked or not. But clients resist changes.

The family comes into therapy because there is a problem. Everyone wants to live a happier, more satisfied life. The mother and, by implication, the others wants Norman to be changed. She tells the therapist her son is unable to make decisions because she wants the therapist to make him able to make decisions. Norman wants to be able to make decisions, in theory, but he also doesn't want to make decisions, because that would mean risking punishment, rejection, and the loss of the satisfactions his mother gives him. Clients give therapists the impression they would like things to be different, while they continue to act in ways which ensure things will stay the same. Therapists term this "resistance." If the therapist were to say, "Norman, make decisions for yourself," Norman obviously wouldn't. The therapist must offer alternative means of meeting Norman's needs that are presently being met by the mother. Can the therapist find a way Norman can be taken care of and protected from his mother? Is this way acceptable to Norman? Is it more acceptable than the status quo?

The therapist is presented with the contradiction: "Help us, but don't change the way we are." Unless, that is, the therapist can satisfy the needs. Unfortunately, therapists cannot meet the needs of their clients. The therapist working with this family cannot protect Norman from his mother (except, perhaps, during sessions), nor can he or she meet Norman's needs for shelter, food, and freedom from responsibility and risk. In short, the family offer themselves to the therapist because they are convinced (unconsciously) that the therapist cannot change things, that things have to be the way they are, even if they are bad. At the same time, the family hopes that therapy will be successful, and things will be better.

Therapy must deal with the demands of the family (or client) for help, even while the resistances to change are expressed in direct or devious ways. To do this the therapist uses techniques or methods which are presented as if they will change the client but which actually leave all changes up to the client. The therapist implies that he or she will do things to make the client better or help the client grow, but instead the therapist only does things which compel the client to make any changes which are necessary and desirable.

Nondirective, client-centered counseling, for example, relies on the reflection of emotions by the therapist as the primary method. Norman may say, "I don't think Mom is justified in putting my girlfriend down. That is, Mom has reasons, she always has reasons for what she does. But in this case if she knew my friend better, she wouldn't feel this way." A nondirective therapist might respond, "You seem to feel resentful toward your mother for not getting to know your friend before making a decision about her." Essentially this response reflects the emotional tone of Norman's indirect complaint about his mother, and Norman would probably say, "Yes, she should get to know her better."

Many clients find nondirective approaches helpful because they feel the therapist "understands" them and often agrees with them. By reflecting the emotions of the client back to him or her, the therapist is validating the client's feelings. In effect the therapist says what the client is saying, but the therapist is taking the risks in expressing the feelings directly. Cli-

THE THIRD PARADOX

The paradox posed by the therapist, in response to the second paradox posed by the client to the therapist, is that the therapist will help (change) the client by saying things which the client will use to realize what he or she wants to change and how to do so. In other words, both nondirective and directive therapists prepare individuals for making the necessary decisions to change things for themselves, while acting as if what the therapist does will cause the changes directly. The client may, and often does, resist interpretations (even nondirective ones may be resisted by the client who fails to generalize from the particular case to the general situation). The therapist, however, is not really doing anything except trying to be helpful by making suggestions. Even angry rebuttals by the client are accepted without any sign of rancor on the part of the therapist, as if the therapist were saying, "I am a therapist. What I do is therapeutic. Even if you are angry and resisting now, later you will be helped. I understand your resistance and accept it because I know you will be better later." In other words, the client is being helped by not being helped to get closer to the point where he or she will be helped. The client might feel that help would be support, affection, expressions of concern, scolding, in short, whatever would make him or her feel better. Feeling better and being helped in psychotherapy are often not the same thing, in the short run.

The therapist changes the definition of "help" within the session as quickly as the client changes the form of resistance he or she uses to prevent change from occurring. At one point, help might be preparing the individual to make decisions, at another, allowing the client to resist help, and finally, allowing the client spontaneously to make changes in his or her life. Help is a mutual agreement between the client and therapist only to the extent that the client stays with therapy (even while missing sessions occasionally). Therapy is a helpful context in which the client tries to demonstrate that the therapist is not helpful and the therapist helps the client by not trying to make direct, explicit changes in the client or the client's situations. On some levels, then, therapy is a relationship between antagonists in a benevolent, helpful arena.

Just as the therapist and client never fully agree on what the problem is, so they never agree on what is helpful. Because it is a therapy relationship the client is expected to perceive *everything* the therapist does or doesn't do as helpful. The therapist never accepts any implication by the client that he or she isn't helpful. The client must contain the contradiction between the therapist's helpfulness and the client's own desire to avoid change. The therapist then widens this split, typically by implying the "unhealthy" side of the client is resisting the "healthy" side, implicitly taking sides with the client against this unhealthy side. The client's attempts to perceive the therapist as the change agent and, therefore, someone to resist are deflected by the therapist's interpretations, questions, or lack of response. The therapist, by acting as if he or she is helpful, compels the client to help himself or herself, thereby being, in fact, helpful.

Essentially the client tries to bind the therapist, to make him or her ineffectual, by using a contradiction between the therapist's behavior and his or her implied or stated intentions. The therapist, avoiding the bind, places the client in a paradoxical situation where even the attempts to bind the therapist are understood by the therapist as part of what is helpful in therapy. For example, if the client attempts to conceal motivations from the therapist by using reasons which are partially true but not central, the therapist understands this as a defense against the emerging emotional content and meaning of the issue. Consequently, the defense is not accepted as a deliberate attempt to mystify the therapist but as a sign of the client's inner conflict, with the therapist remaining objective and neutral. It is the neutrality or lack of response to provocations and resistances which ultimately defeats the client. Everything he or she does to confound the therapist and prevent change is made to appear as if it is leading to those changes. The binding process is reversed, with the client within a paradox he or she can only resolve through acting in a different and acceptable manner. Should the client act differently, but in a way the therapist still considers a symptom, the client is acting out rather than maturing; this new behavior is focused on as the development of the problem leading to a solution but not as a solution. Successful termination in therapy comes when the client makes spontaneous changes, which result from therapy but not from anything the therapist did.

THE FOURTH PARADOX

How does a client change because of therapy? How is he or she helped? The final part of our answer to these questions is the fourth paradox. There are two versions to this paradox, and I think they are both important. The first approach stresses the overall goal of the therapist to help the client by increasing his or her insight and emotional awareness. The second stresses the goals of the client, and the therapist bases interventions on these goals, trying to effect immediate changes congruent with these goals.

Most therapists would view the family in much the same way. They would agree on the dynamics, perhaps stressing some things more than others. Recently there has been a move away from an exclusive reliance on one-to-one therapy relationships, and more emphasis is placed on dealing with the family as a system. Despite the range of methods from nondirective therapy to directive techniques like gestalt therapy and psychodrama, where a considerable amount of the client's participation in therapy is under the direction of the therapist, the emphasis in therapy is largely on creating the necessary prerequisites—insight and emotional awareness—for personal change.

Consequently, regardless of the method the family members or an individual client would be guided by the therapist's intervention toward understanding, the integration of insight with emotions. Interpretations would suggest or state connections the client is unaware of between events and ideas, ideas, events and emotions, and so forth. Even when the body is a primary focus, the effort is to release repressed emotions and to change the body so it is less easy to store feelings the individual has never recognized and accepted. If the therapist goes beyond verbal interactions (questions, suggestions, advice, interpretations, responses) and creates specific, structured situations like a psychodrama, the hot seat in gestalt therapy, or a group environment, the emphasis is still primarily on insight and emotions.

The basic assumption is that when Norman, Terri, the mother, and the father have greater understanding of their family and themselves, they will spontaneously make changes in their lives which will be authentic and creative. Insight and unrepressed emotions are considered necessary for personal changes of any magnitude to occur. Many therapists, ideologically committed to objectivity, would decry any suggestion that they have goals for the clients. Few would acknowledge that they want Norman and Terri to move out and be independent; they want the mother and father to redefine their marriage so it becomes satisfying for both and so the mother won't be on the kids' backs.

The family, then, having explicit although narrow goals, is responded to by the therapist in a way which resolves neither the presenting problem nor any of the other levels of difficulty which emerge in the course of therapy. This binds the client. The client, remember, has been trying to get the therapist to commit himself or herself to a specific attempt to change the client in order to defeat the therapist, despite, paradoxically, the client's desire to change something to relieve his or her anguish—to be helped.

The paradoxical bind placed on the client is not crippling, any more than any other double bind we have described, because there are alternatives to the client which will be positive and satisfying. According to the general assumptions made about this approach, the client can resolve the bind by doing one of four things. First, as the therapist is doing something, the client can wait and see what the something is leading to. By cooperating the client does achieve insight and emotional awareness: there is no need to resist either strenuously since the therapist continually assures the client that he or she need do nothing but think and feel.

Recently a therapist described to me a situation in which she was able to make a major breakthrough with a client. He had worn a piece of clothing associated, unconsciously, with his feelings of resentment toward his father, a major issue in his attempts to define his own identity. The therapist observed the clothing and commented on the connection as a plausible one. The man exploded in anger. He subsided when the therapist insisted that he didn't have to change anything, just think about what the meaning might be. This is a paradoxical instruction, because doing nothing and thinking are contradictions. The man realized that his attempt to defeat the therapist was unnecessary; she was not trying to change him. Yet she did suggest something which he didn't usually do: to think about the meaning of that piece of clothing. To do this he had to consider why he wore the clothing that day, a day when he made a particularly successful presentation at work.

By being open to learning, that is, in attempting to think and feel, the client is doing two things he or she is rarely aware of: one is making a slight change in his or her usual pattern (which implies the possibility of making other changes in other patterns), and the other is doing so in response to the therapist's interventions (establishing a pattern of cooperating with therapy). After many months of repeating these changes, often totally unrelated to the specific problems, the client becomes used to following a new pattern, making changes, and doing so in response to therapy.

Therapy is a helping relationship. In that context the client knows that continued participation in therapy should be helpful. Furthermore, the therapist doesn't try to make direct changes, only to increase the client's understanding. The client eventually uses this understanding to make changes, since there is no alternative as long as he or she is in therapy. The client, in cooperating with therapy and in seeing therapy as helpful, eventually has to make "spontaneous" decisions to change whatever is involved with his or her problems. The therapist has prepared the client by creating nonthreatening, seemingly unconnected patterns; the possibility of change is established, as is the notion the client is cooperating with therapy, not with the therapist.

This is the most positive response to the therapist's bind. The client can also perceive that interpretations, suggestions, questions are leading somewhere. After repeated attempts to find out where fail, with the therapist persistently saying that he or she has no goals for the client and is trying to remain objective, the client may resort to repression of the therapist. This involves undermining the therapist by a refusal to generalize from any specific idea to a larger class of related ideas or persistent reluctance to experience emotions except under the guidance of the therapist (then with defensive responses). This extremely suspicious attitude is usually in response to a therapist who is, in fact, leading the client to a particular point of view or action with an embarrassing transparency.

A young girl of fifteen was placed in therapy by her parents. She was unwilling to remain in school, although when she ran away from home or school it was never overnight. She was eager to have sexual relations with her boyfriend but was conflicted over the relative inexperience of the boy. She wasn't sure if they could get it together successfully. Her therapist was unconsciously (or at least he evidenced no awareness of being) against her having intercourse. He persisted in making interpretations like, "What you would really like to do is be closer to your father," or, "Just because other girls do it, do you think this means you must?" His first statement assumes that her desire to be close to her father is directly related to her wanting to make love. She assumed it was because she was horny, wanted to know what sex was like, and liked the boy. His second statement implies that sexual desire in her is a compulsion occasioned by a desire to conform to other girls. She knew her friends weren't having sex, and she resented the idea that it wasn't her choice to make love.

The unskilled therapist who makes biases explicit opens the relationship up for the client to defeat the goals. This is particularly true when the values and ideology of the therapist are at odds with those of the client. As a client you know when the therapist approves or disapproves of things, particularly if you see the therapist over time. A therapist has to be very unresponsive and remote for this not to happen, and clients often find this fearful, making them suspicious of the therapist and simultaneously obsessed with what the therapist is like. Obsession serves to keep the client stabilized: there is no change.

A third way of dealing with the fourth paradox is to reject the therapy context as helpful. By rejecting the context the client doesn't have to follow an implicit injunction that therapy per se is helpful. Many people, for instance, reject established agencies and, by association, the therapist. Even when they accept an individual therapist, they continue to reject and fear the institution. There is no injunction to get better; although they might develop insight and emotional awareness, they do not make significant changes in their lives. Often the therapy is terminated, while both the therapist and client forget the presenting problem and fail to resolve underlying issues. After all, therapists assume that insight and emotional awareness are basic prerequisites for change. Clients with insight and emotional awareness are frequently clients a second, third, or fourth time, always agreeing they were helped, but with basic problems still left unresolved. A client may be qualitatively better off with insight and awareness, better able to cope with situation, but still stuck.

A fourth resolution of the bind is not to have major problems in the first place. Clients who see therapy as a personal growth experience, rather than as a problem-solving situation, need not have major changes in their personalities, lifestyles, or situations. They can learn from therapy and be fundamentally satisfied and encouraged to continue learning in other relationships. One might say that they already have the prerequisite for learning—a life without major problems with which they are deeply involved but over which they experience little control.

The form of the fourth paradox we have been discussing is often helpful to people who are not strongly committed to defending against change (that is, not very disturbed or crazy) or who do not need or want fundamental changes, but who do want to learn about themselves and their relationships with other people. The quality of therapy, the relative degrees of helpfulness, will then depend on what the therapist is able to bring to the situation, what metaphors or contrived experiences are used to discuss issues, and what skills the therapist has in facilitating the resolution of the four paradoxes. Typically therapy is not helpful to very disturbed people—those heavily committed to stability, the absence of change—or to people who are ideologically (politically) alienated from the context. This group includes women, minority group members, homosexuals and lesbians, and some schizophrenics.

An alternative to orthodox goals has been developed for both groups. The first approach is extremely directive, attempting to meet the long-range goals of the client immediately (that is, according to the first model, what clients might do after they develop insight and emotional awareness). The second approach attempts to analyze the basic concepts of established therapy and create alternatives with a political awareness: it is radical therapy, which will eventually lead to contexts for therapy fundamentally different from the existing ones.

The directive approach views the presenting problem as the immediate goal of therapy. Unlike traditional approaches, which make major changes long-range goals and prefer to emphasize insight and emotional awareness, direct approaches deal with the symptom as the problem. I believe there is a sophisticated and a naïve alternative offered here. The naïve alternative is behavioral modification, which, through a series of rewards, punishment, and exposure to tabooed areas, attempts to modify the particular symptom. But behavioral modification lacks awareness of the underlying issues. I don't believe that the removal of a symptom will only lead to another symptom; there is no evidence for this. But I do believe symptoms are not only problems in themselves, but are related to a specific problematic area the individual might be content to live with (without symptom formation) but which therapy could bring out and deal with so the client wouldn't have to live with it.

In our family example, Norman could be worked with on the basis of the symptom. By being moved out of the house and placed in a residential program which rewarded initiative and decision making, while ignoring or punishing the lack of decision making (perhaps through constant confrontation, making decision making more pleasant than continually putting up with crap), Norman could probably be changed. But the method overlooks the value of Norman's behavior as a way of calling attention to the dilemma of the entire family.

Furthermore, the changes are not spontaneous and, therefore, are not necessarily integrated into the personality so they can be used in analogous situations the client may get into in the future. No learning has taken place; the client has simply been trained to perform in socially acceptable ways. This may be enough for people who merely want to get over smoking, impotence, frigidity, drinking, homosexual desires, and so forth. In many cases overcoming a symptom can be a major and highly valuable thing to do, whatever method is used.

Another highly directive technique or approach is to create a fourth paradox for the client by defining contradictions which compel the client, regardless of what he or she does, to make a significant change. If the problem is complicated, a series of fourth paradoxes may be necessary, the cumulative effect being a spontaneous, undirected choice which resolves the problematic situation.

I would approach Norman's family as follows. First,

I would listen to the mother outline the problems as she sees them and find out what the others think are the problems. Then I would say something like, "I can help you with your problems as a family." This emphasis would suggest that the family is troubled, rather than that just one person has something wrong with him or her. The emphasis is true, since everyone in the family agrees that Norman's inability to make decisions is a problem for the whole family as well as for him. It also includes unspecified, perhaps unmentioned problems, which, I imply, I expect my approach to help.

Second, I might tell them, "Therapy is an extremely difficult process, with many problems involved, creating unpleasant feelings; yet this is necessary for change to occur." By stressing the difficulties I am able to say without contradiction that therapy involves change. Furthermore, I am deliberately ambiguous. Are the difficulties a result of therapy or the basis for seeking therapy or both? Since I don't intend to focus on these questions, they only serve to keep the family off balance, unsure as to what to expect and therefore open to suggestion.[2]

Third, I usually ask them for a commitment: "Will you all agree to go through with therapy, even though it will become difficult, in order for me to help you with all your problems?" Since Norman and the others have been brought in by the mother, I want each to make an agreement with me to go through therapy with me. I put "difficult" between the commitment and the end result, help, deliberately, so they will

[2]My approach is similar to that of Milton Erickson's, although I arrived at it by different means. See Jay Haley, *Uncommon Therapy: The Psychiatric Techniques of Milton H. Erickson, M.D.* (New York: Norton, 1973).

know that when things do get difficult, help is near. Of course each agrees. Things can't be more difficult, they think, than they already are: they came into therapy because things were so bad. Besides, expecting things to get worse and braving them as expectations is heroic and easy. Now that the contract is made, at least initially, therapy can begin.

My fourth move, if there is any hesitation, is to suggest they go home and think it over. With this mother behind the idea of therapy there will be no hesitation, because she is too powerful. Now I am ready to create a bind for Norman, which he will not be able to get out of without making a decision. Yet at the same time I want him to expand the decision to other areas, and I want it all to be spontaneous. Consequently, I direct my next statements to the mother.

"You came in here because you are worried about your family. You have a very close family." So far there is nothing to disagree with, and she even acknowledges the "compliment" most people would perceive as a sign of something wrong considering the ages of her children. "You brought them in here because something is wrong, and you want to be helpful. Bringing them here was helpful." This supports the mother more. She is expecting a sting by this time; no one has ever supported her this much without a price, and she is wondering what my price is. "You want me to help them with you." She nods. Here I have anticipated her attempts to control me and become the therapist by suggesting that any such attempts will be construed as helping me, not preventing me from being helpful. "You want to know how you can help your son make decisions for himself and how you can help Terri act more maturely." This is essentially the same thing, because both children need to grow up.

The mother senses the children are immature and dependent. Part of her likes this and has done everything possible to see that they remain dependent. The other part of her is worried: something is wrong, and she knows what it is. Her children are still at home and don't seem prepared ever to take care of themselves. This frightens her, since she wants the best for them. She also wants to be the one to decide what is best. These inferences are based on the therapy dialogue but for the sake of space are asserted.

"Obviously they need to be taken care of." This is a truth they didn't expect me to say. It again takes everyone off guard. The mother believes they need to be taken care of, or she wouldn't have any justification for controlling them. She asserts this belief by disparaging everything they do for themselves. It is obviously inferior and inadequate, definite proof of their need for her. "Adults who don't need to be taken care of by their mother usually leave home." This is a slam at the children but is a generally accepted fact at the same time. By saying usually I leave open the possibility that some mature people remain home. Besides, each feels he or she does need to be taken care of, or they would be fighting the mother tooth and nail.

But I have also suggested that leaving home is a sign of not being taken care of anymore. Up to this time the mother has balanced her control efforts with lots of satisfaction of needs. The children get free room, board, clothes, and spending money, while being free to come and go (in a car the mother bought the son). In return they are obedient and manipulative. The only source of friction is the fact that Norman's friend is being rejected by the mother.

"I think you, as their mother, need to help them make decisions for themselves even more than you already have, so they can learn to make decisions for themselves and become independent. They won't need to be taken care of anymore." Here is the first part of the contradiction. The mother is being told to be more controlling, since being controlling hasn't worked. She is allowed to continue believing that controlling children is the proper way to bring up children. Hence, she is open to the suggestion rather than defensive: there will be no fundamental change, only more of the same. Yet this unbalances the situation at home, making the mother more intrusive, consequently more frustrating. Norman and Terri will have to cope with the frustration. They will probably take it out on the mother.

"Of course, when children are being difficult" (there is the promised difficulty for the mother and for the children) "as they sometimes are when decisions are being made for them, it might be necessary to take away some of their privileges." This sticks the kids. First, I refer to them as children, the way they act and probably think of themselves. But it still makes them mad at me. I want them to be mad at me so they don't hear the second part of the statement about their "privileges." I then outline the areas where she has to lay it right on the line, including whatever she feels the father needs to do to shape up. "You have to set an example." Since this is generally the role of a father, he really can't object. "Of course, things can go back to normal once Norman and Terri are willing to make decisions for themselves." Now I have offered him a bribe: get the kids out of the house, and your wife will get off your back. Let them stay, and I'll keep her after you too. This involves the father, for the first time in a long time, however indirectly, in the raising of his children.

The mother's energy and her skills at being controlling are now assisting me in therapy. Motivated by the well-being of her children, she is going to drive them out of the nest. Yet she will not want them to leave. I must put her in a bind similar to that of her children. They have two alternatives: stay home and suffer a controlling mother coupled with a loss of privileges or get out on their own. The father and mother are both going to be driving them out.

"It seems to me," I say to the father, "that you have virtually left home. You are there to eat and sleep but find your work keeps you away the rest of the time." Now I am dealing with the marital problems. "Perhaps you can use some help from your wife." This brings it back to the mother, who I can count on to want to nourish somebody (that's her pattern) soon, since I will shortly have her taking things away from the kids. "Why don't you start doing things especially nice for your husband. As your relationship improves because of therapy you will want to be closer." This implies that the children will be leaving and the parents will have to be closer to survive the loss. It also indicates that I think focusing on the difficulties she has with her husband will occur as a part of the therapy relationship. "Of course, as you have explained, you have difficulty expressing your anger to your husband. Perhaps as the situation arises you can practice with someone less threatening." Now the kids will catch hell on top of everything else. She will also learn to feel comfortable with hostility and anger, since the only effect will be to drive the kids out, which is the natural function of a family (perhaps accomplished in this case in an unusual manner). This will be a positive result, since the mother can avoid seeing her anger as the cause for their leaving.

Rather, she can see their leaving as a success plateau for her as a mother. Besides, she's being drained by the kids and father. No one is supporting her.

"The relationship will change," I continue, talking to no one in particular. Then I turn to the father. "As long as your wife will be making things comfortable at home, perhaps you can tell her some of what you would like." This is the first time father can tell mother anything, and she has to listen in order to take care of him, making her own life more secure. "Perhaps you can show her, by doing special things for her you also like for yourself." This allows the father to take initiative and have his wife cooperate. I suggest they go home and sit down and talk with each other about how they can each make the home more comfortable. This will give the father an opportunity to discuss what he likes and doesn't like about how his wife treats him and have her listen (she has to so she will know what to do to get him home more).

I explicitly ignore the two children, giving them no direct instructions whatsoever. No matter what they do, they will be caught in a bind they can only resolve by deciding to leave home and take care of themselves. The longer they stay, the less they will get out of the family situation. If they need more urging, I will begin interfering, through the mother, in Norman's sex life, which is his major outside commitment, all the while suggesting how much more he could enjoy a sexual relationship if he lived somewhere else. By tantalizing both with imagined pleasures of independent living and real frustrations if they maintain their present status, I will maximize the attractiveness of the solution. At no time would I suggest they move out, and my suggestions about how pleasant it would be will refer to other people, as if my speculations have nothing to do with Norman and Terri.

The remaining sessions are used to magnify the contradictions in the family. Norman and Terri moved out shortly, although each continued in therapy, working on problems of being independent. The mother appeared less controlling, more supportive, and therefore less alienating to the father who came home more often. There was no easy relationship; they didn't know each other well. Some families and clients prefer the longer approach, but this family did well in brief treatment.

One point worth mentioning in connection with this example is the therapist's apparent support for a stereotypic role for the mother. Starting with the premise that the therapist's primary task is to accept people where they are and help them become what they want to become or achieve what they want to achieve in their lives, rather than imposing ideological values (whatever the justification), the therapist noted that the mother wanted the husband to be home more. He suggested ways she could achieve this goal. First, by expressing her anger more directly to him, even if she first displaces it onto the children in order to learn to be more comfortable with aggression, the woman will be less tense, repressed, and frustrated—less terrified of her husband. Next, by listening to what he wants (and thus forcing the husband to say what he wants for the first time) she can learn how to make her home more comfortable for him, and consequently for herself. Of course, once he begins listing demands openly, she will be free to weigh the demands against her own desires to see if they are things with which she wants to comply. Finally, by redefining his own satisfaction and recreation to include his wife, the father must find out what his wife wants from him, to do with him. Instead of being nagged or bombarded with demands, he must seek her out. Suggesting the woman join a group would have met with disbelief and distrust by this woman (however helpful such a group might have been). She didn't want her ideas about being a mother and a wife to be challenged; what she did want was more satisfaction in her relationships. Later, however, the idea of group therapy might make more sense to her and in anything but short term therapy would be explored.

Helpfulness in psychotherapy comes from the heightened awareness of contradictions in a person's life which he or she must ultimately do something to resolve. The techniques of the therapist may facilitate the helping process or retard it. Or the techniques may create contradictions in the therapy relationship which usually hurt the clients. Certainly contradictions in therapy delay change. Regardless of what the therapist's goals are, spontaneous, independent choices by the client are the preferred outcome.

Along the way, clients may learn a great deal about themselves. Through the clarification of their problems, heightened awareness of contradictions in their lives, exploration of issues and themes and their implications to other areas tangentially related to the primary difficulties clients find the quality of understanding is deepened. Furthermore, by sorting out their feelings (which they learn to acknowledge, appreciate, and express), clients are able to become centered. They are not tossed about in conflicts like a leaf in the wind. If therapists use metaphors beyond the problems or stories the clients present, such as psychodramas, photographs, drawings, painting, dreams, group experience, and so forth, the vocabularies of clients are enriched. They are able to speak in different languages about their concerns, to express themselves creatively and freely.

But the rewards of therapy beyond personal changes to cope with the painful contradictions in the clients' lives are not, in themselves, helpful. They add dimension and quality to change processes when change is occuring, not trivial changes which many people make just because they are alive, but changes in the contradictions causing anguish, confusion, and frustration. The changes clients find helpful will ultimately be the ones they make in their own situations because therapy has made continual sufferance of the contradictions undesirable. Through experiencing the four basic paradoxes of therapy clients begin, almost in the first session, to prepare themselves to make these changes. At best, the therapist stays out of the way.

7

Getting out of Therapy

"Getting out of therapy" may be understood in two ways: getting out of therapy what you want, or, if you are not getting what you want, then getting the hell out of therapy.

You can always get out of therapy. Anyone who remains in a therapy situation which is noxious, for whatever reason, is asking for trouble. Leaving therapy is not a sign of failure; it is a way of taking care of yourself. If you felt the therapist were taking care of you, why would you feel like leaving? Ordinarily people leave therapy for valid reasons; I think they always leave for valid reasons.

Doria went through a phase of being very seductive toward a remote father, who never responded to her needs except when she coyly attracted his sexual interest and flattered his ego. After leaving home, Doria, no longer prohibited by the incest taboo from merely acting seductive, became quite promiscuous. This led to despair. Men were not responding to her needs, although by this time her need was too much for anyone to fulfill. Doria concluded that her satisfaction could come only through men, and continual disappointment led her to look for other alternatives. She began drinking. Being an alcoholic was even more frustrating, humiliating, and filled with despair than being promiscuous.

Doria stopped drinking and turned instead to her husband for support. She was becoming stronger, but he acted toward her as if she were weak. When she became angry, he patronized her. By never becoming angry in response and fighting with her, which would have validated her anger, he became "understanding." By implying the problem was her feelings of powerlessness and frustration and other deficiencies in Doria, he escaped responsibility as a source of her anger. Doria felt helpless and guilty for being angry at a kind and understanding husband. She became increasingly disturbed, finally seeking therapy for a third time. In therapy Doria thought, appropriately, she would find some validation for the idea that her frustrations were in some ways the result of her relationship with her husband and not entirely manifestations of her deficiencies as a person. Furthermore, she hoped the therapist would help her meet her needs.

The therapist recognized the anger and tried to deal with the anger Doria felt toward him by accepting it but asking why Doria was angry. She had to explain her anger. This is one interpretation of the thrust toward insight. He didn't become angry, outwardly, at her incessant demands on him. He acted as if he had anger under control, so by implication Doria was out of control. Doria was furious and helpless again. In this case, because the therapist responded by asking questions and making interpretations about the sources of her anger, he was putting Doria in a bind. If she were to feel anger, she would have to accept total responsibility for it. This would mean repressing the anger so it was under control and accepting both her husband and the therapist as helpful, sympathetic men: in other words, giving up her own perceptions that somehow they didn't validate her anger, accept her right just to be furious.

Eventually, as Doria continued to be furious, the

therapist shifted the focus of the sessions. She was "resisting insight," and perhaps if he focused on other issues, she would become less defensive. Ignoring her anger as just more of the same fury, the therapist began to focus on her relationship with her husband, not in terms of what he did to her but, avoiding this, in terms of what she wanted from him. Again Doria had to justify needing, rather than looking at what her husband and the therapist did to frustrate her needs indirectly.

She begins talking about a confusion in her mind between the therapist and her husband. She thinks she is falling in love with the therapist, and when she makes love to her husband, she thinks of the therapist. The therapist, happy to be away from the anger that is still evident in her avoidance of his eyes, her tense position, and the striking of her hand against the chair, accepts this by asking more questions and occasionally relating things she says to other incidents in her life. He does this in a gentle, soft voice, making his voice gentler and softer the more irritated Doria acts.

Although the therapist has no thought of actually going to bed with Doria, he is, in fact, seducing her. Through his willingness to talk about sexuality and his avoidance of both her demands on him and her fury at being rejected, he is encouraging her to focus on only the sexual elements of her relationship with him. Obligingly she begins having fantasies. He is naïve enough to realize she is indifferent, unresponsive, and distant from her husband while making love and uses her fantasies to avoid the experience of sex. Now she is putting the therapist into the fantasies, making her coldness his responsibility. Furthermore, she is implicitly saying that the therapist is causing her to have fantasies, so she can later dump her anger on him for rejecting her. This is a paradoxical way of going out of her way to end up where she already is, coping with the therapist's rejection of her and her fury. Will the therapist be able to talk about his rejection of her, which he has not yet directly acknowledged as the reasonable interpretation of his rejecting her demands to meet her needs, indirectly through the metaphor of sexuality. This gives him an out. He can obviously and ethically turn down her request to go to bed and talk about this directly.

Doria, an experienced client, is putting the therapist in a bind where he will have to help her by talking about his rejection of her demands. Doria wants to know why men always seem to reject her demands to meet needs she believes men should meet and probably do for other women. Her self-contempt, reinforced by both her husband's and the therapist's benevolence and sympathy toward her fury, is being increasingly reinforced. But the problem is, why does Doria have to put the therapist in a bind to get him to help her?

The bias of this therapist is toward "objective" participation. In other words, no matter what the client does, remain soft, quiet, gentle, and unresponsive. Continue making interpretations or asking questions, but never deal with implicit or direct demands except by inquiring into their source. Doria doesn't want this from her therapist: she gets it from her husband. And she withdraws from his affection now because she can't trust her husband's emotions. He doesn't even realize when she's thinking of someone else while he is making love to her. Her husband uses her and fails to confront her. Yet she is seduced into the relationship because it is the primary source of warmth, support, and concern in her life. Now she is being seduced by her therapist who acts just like her husband and doesn't really become involved with her as a person.

The consistency of this therapist's style may eventually lead Doria or women who are in the same bind to a resolution of the bind, probably because his ritualized, automatic responses are making him vulnerable to her binds on him to reject her and give her something definite to work on. It is more likely, however, that Doria will fail. The therapist will not reject her, he will only say he doesn't want to make love to her and is not becoming involved with her and cannot, even if he wanted to, because it would be unethical. He will not admit to wanting to or, more likely, wanting to be seen as wanting to. He would have to see that his consistently supportive warmth, gentleness, and acceptance of whatever Doria does is seductive. It promises an intimacy that is not there and won't be there. And he presents himself as a person who never gets angry or rejecting or punitive or appears not to, while Doria experiences him as rejecting.

In other words, the therapist can step out of Doria's bind on him by denying the elements of the contradiction. He can say, "I don't want to love you, only to help you. If you want to make love with me or fall in love with me, that is in your own head." This throws the absurdity of the fantasies back into Doria's head, making her entirely responsible for her response to the therapy relationship, as if the therapist did not give her any cues at all. Doria will not improve in this relationship. She will be unable to resolve her two primary problems. The first is her assumption that men can and should meet all her needs (which are felt but unspecific), if she only can find a way of making them (they don't *really* like her enough freely to satisfy her). The second, is her attraction to men who appear to be able to meet her needs (gentle, soft, supportive) but who constantly invalidate her anger, demands, and reactions to their unresponsiveness with paternal understanding and by denying any involvement in creating the negative feelings.

Doria is perceived by her therapist as resistant to change, despite the fact that she has worked through promiscuity, alcoholism, and other dependencies in the last four years. Actually, she is a prime client, having demonstrated a great deal of strength and resolve. Therapy would be greatly enhanced by the therapist stating, as a starting point, "Look, you are a very strong person. Only a very strong person could handle dependencies like you have and outgrown them. Yet here you sit whining and complaining. You are furious with me, with men. Your father never liked you and only responded when you were cute and pretty. He didn't want to know about the rest of you: the part that becomes angry, demanding, and ugly, particularly when you don't get what you want. You looked to other men, but they just used you too, having no interest in you as a real person who makes demands on men because you think they have something you need. You became so frustrated and felt so much a failure you turned to alcohol. That didn't make you any better. So you stopped; it was hard, but you did it. Now your husband doesn't want to hear that you are angry with him. He doesn't want to look at what he does you don't like: how remote he is from you. He can even make love to you without being involved enough in you to make you want to be with him. You fantasize about me or someone else or about him, the way you would like him to be. Now, look, let's get some things straight. I can help you, but I won't and don't want to meet your needs. I don't even know what you want, and I don't think you do either. If we knew, perhaps we could go about finding a way for you to get what you want. Let's look at all the ways you try to trick me into satisfying your needs and all the ways the men you know, probably including me, find ways of not doing what you want. For example, what do you want from your husband? For him to let you be angry and not blame this anger on you but to look at what he does you are angry about? What does he do? Things like making love to your body but ignoring your mind?"

This approach, summed up in a monologue, would accomplish several things. First, Doria would be supported. She is strong, able to take care of herself, to get herself out of real difficulties, to find out what she wants, to find ways of making people listen to what she wants. Second, the two major patterns in her life, which continually cause her to suffer unresolvable contradictions, are specified: her attempts to do anything which will make men listen to her demands, needs, and feelings based on the false belief that men can meet her needs if she can trick them into doing it rather than meeting her needs herself by finding out what she wants and how to ask for it and being sure she gets it (by clarifying what she wants, the unrealistic demands will be obvious and will be discarded after a while) and her misperception of men that causes her to think that because a man appears warm, supportive, and gentle he is, despite her own experiences of men as rejecting and frustrating. She is mystified. The therapist suggests that every man is to some extent frustrating and rejecting, even he.

Third, the response would give her something to work on with the therapist. By using questions, interpretations, and responses, the therapist has given her a frame of reference to learn in, to experiment with, and to use as a way of interpreting her whole life.

Fourth, the therapist would be really with her, recognizing her anger, the reasons for it in her and in the people she knows, and her strengths. As a whole person in the eyes of the therapist, she can begin reevaluating her self-contempt. ("If the therapist thinks I'm strong because I did stop being promiscuous, did stop drinking, and do want to change, why don't I?") Fifth, the therapist clarifies the nature of the therapy relationship. He will help her find ways of solving her problems, including looking at the way he and others contribute to the problems. She can get angry with him, and he'll listen! He'll look at what he is doing; he will not undermine her perceptions and intuition, nor will he seduce her by using her needs as a way of making her believe he will and can meet them.

The difference between these two responses has been set down to show that some therapists, with good intentions, do not help clients. By contrasting the two approaches, both of which have value in certain contexts with particular people, I have shown how one therapist, in doing what he always does, is helpful, and another is hurtful. If this woman were alert enough, she would be able to see what she feels: the therapist is like her husband; he is not like a therapist. He is cuing her to seek a relationship in fantasy which will only lead to rejection and possibly to a realization that she has to change her idea of the therapist in order to find out what he is really likely to do. Why should this woman go through all this difficulty to learn something as ambiguous and unhelpful as "you were wrong to love me." The risk taking is predicated on the belief that whatever the therapist does will eventually, at some point in the future, help.

I think this is a weak premise on which to continue a therapy relationship, considering the emotional stresses involved. I think clients should be able to demand that their therapists be helpful in the session now, rather than hoping for a good outcome. That doesn't mean expecting instant cures, but it does mean expecting a clear, precise, concrete relationship, which minimizes ambiguities and offers the client a satisfactory means of participation. Some clients like to do all the talking, others want a responsive therapist. Neither type should settle for a therapy that is not what they want.

The final judgment about the effectiveness of therapy is up to you, the client. Give up this judgment to the therapist, and you are in peril. You are depending too much on the judgment of the therapist about your needs and desires. You can negotiate with many therapists. Criticizing an approach or an attitude—no one is always on top of the situation, always feeling good, always responding well—should help you and the therapist come to terms with noxious elements in therapy. If the situation cannot be negotiated and the stress and confusion builds up to the point where the relationship with the therapist becomes the primary focus of your stress and not your problems, leave.

The decision to leave therapy will almost always be to your advantage, not to your disadvantage. Staying when you are having more trouble with the therapist will usually be to your disadvantage. In Doria's case her therapist was unintentionally leading her into her bind. But as she begins to concentrate on her relationship with him, she should be able to realize, "Hey, I went to him with problems, not for problems." At that point she could say, "Why should I have these difficulties over you? Either straighten out the ambiguities creating my confusion, or I'm going to go to another therapist." One doesn't have to leap to the threat; in fact, leaving should not be a threat to the therapist. A therapist should be able to accept the fact that some clients are helped by him or her, and others are not. The therapist who needs a client to continue is not being either helpful or truthful to himself or herself.

The right to leave, the ability to leave, is the primary source of protection for the client. Few clients entering therapy are able to take all they should into consideration: the orientation of the therapy (personal growth, treatment, crisis intervention, problem solving), the therapist (personality, style, politics), the methods (experiential, verbal, physical, mixed), what the therapist perceives help to be, and so forth. But anyone is able to leave a session, or not to come back for more.

The therapy relationship is highly personal. One has the right to make and trust subjective decisions about how helpful or unhelpful the therapy relationship is. In Doria's case she might talk with friends or even another therapist about a decision to leave. But would they notice that the therapist was cultivating her bind, unintentionally, by doing what many therapists do as a matter of course? They probably would not, so relying on outside opinions isn't always a way of being sure. Furthermore, Doria undoubtedly would feel better as a result of this therapy relationship, even though she might not be helped. She would feel better because she releases pent-up emotions, perhaps allowing repressed emotions closer to the surface, gains some insight, and will feel, to some extent, liked by the therapist. Making a decision between feeling better and being helped is a difficult one: change involves emotional stress, and therapy which only makes you feel better is probably not helpful in changing the basic dilemmas.

The difficulty of knowing why you want to leave should not keep anyone from leaving: you can rely on intuition. If your attitude changes after having left, or you feel prepared to cope with the stresses leading to a sudden exit better, you can always return or go to another therapist and another. The overall similarity between many therapists' approaches and styles as therapists, because of the unfortunate ritualization of therapy encouraged by graduate schools and clinical institutions, may mean that an intensive search is necessary.

Some people, having abruptly left therapy, decide they must cope with reality on their own. They decide that life has problems, not just that they have problems so life seems difficult. Reality problems, for example, finding meaningful employment, raising children, living a viable lifestyle, relationships with other people, are just there, regardless of what stage a person is in. Therapy can release the person caught up in binds and unable to make changes or respond to changes, but the reality problems remain. They never go away, and people who hope they will if they just go to therapy long enough are bound to be disappointed.

Going into therapy is a difficult decision to make. Once in, people tend to stay. Perhaps this is ordinarily acceptable, since many people do not want or demand effective therapy as long as they have someone to talk with who appears to be listening. Others find the insight and emotional awareness sufficiently supportive to allow them to accept binds which may eventually drop away for reasons outside of the control of the client or the therapist. Some find therapy helpful, and real changes are made. Others look for effective psychotherapy and may want to explore approaches which are not based entirely on insight and emotional awareness. Many people want a great deal more, including personal growth experiences. Others want to escape themselves or a hurtful relationship.

After coming to terms with the decisions you make about therapy and if you find therapy an unpleasant experience, you can leave. If you find therapy helpful or simply at an end, you can leave. Going into therapy necessitates, for whatever reasons, getting out of therapy. Decisions about therapy are important to you. Why not make as many of them as you can yourself?

75 76 77 78 79 10 9 8 7 6 5 4 3 2 1